# DARKNESS AT DAWN
A journey of hope, healing
and forgiveness

**Darrell and Sherri Beebe
with Karen Koczwara**

Published in Beaverton, Oregon, by Good Catch Publishing.
www.goodcatchpublishing.com
V1.1

*Printed in the United States of America*

# Table of Contents

# DEDICATION

"… We also rejoice in our sufferings, because we know that suffering produces perseverance; perseverance, character; and character, hope. And hope does not disappoint us, because God has poured out His love into our hearts by the Holy Spirit, whom He has given us." (Romans 5:3-5)

With love and admiration, we dedicate this book to our children, Jeremy and Jadie, who persevered through suffering to become examples of godly character and hope. You are an inspiration to us and to others.
We are so proud of you.

# SPECIAL THANKS

Enormous thanks and special blessings to Jennifer (Kiesser) Beebe and David Hager. They say you can't pick your family, but Jeremy and Jadie richly blessed our family when they chose these special people as their life mates.

Although they were not with us in the beginning of our story, our long journey to healing was very much a part of their lives. We honor them for embracing and loving who we were and, with their love and support, who we have become.

Heartfelt appreciation goes to our dear friends Steve and Virginia Bjorklund. They offered us friendship as we married. They have walked through deep valleys in their own lives and still they have always been available to encourage and help us on our journey to freedom.

We also want to thank everyone who has lifted us up in prayer prior to and after our trauma.

Words cannot describe how much your prayers and encouragement to write our story has meant to us.

# INTRODUCTION

**Darrell**

"I will never forgive them. They ruined my life!"

These words always get my attention when watching the news. Another innocent life taken and a family is, by no wrong choice of their own, thrown into the public arena where every feeling and emotion is on display.

One doesn't have to live very long to learn that life isn't fair. We live in a world where people hurt people, and hurt people hurt people. No doubt you have been hurt by what someone has said or done to you. It is not *if* we are going to get hurt by people. It's when. Sometimes the wrong choices of others only affect them. Other times, their wrong choices affect our lives, too. Forever.

When this happens, we have one of two choices to make: We can respond or we can react. Our family chose to respond and not to react. We refused to become victims to the past bad actions of others. We chose to become better and not bitter.

It would be nice to say that this was a quick and easy process, but the truth is, it was not. Because of the wrong choices of three men, our entire life was laid waste.

Dealing with the consequences of their actions, we found ourselves struggling with fear, anger, hatred and thoughts of revenge. Our sleep was interrupted with reoccurring thoughts of the attack. Our faith and trust in God was put to the test as we learned how to allow the truth of God's word to affect every part of our lives and bring peace and freedom.

**Sherri**

Some stories can be written in a day. Others take a lifetime. This book has been more than 20 years in the making. This is not just the story of one night of terror. This is the story of the long, tough process of healing through forgiving.

We have a choice in our response to tragedy. God desires to give every story a "happy ending." He is carefully weaving golden threads into our life's tapestry.

When we moved our family to the Pacific Islands in 1984, we had our own ideas of the storyline the experience would write into our lives. It certainly did not include terror, trauma and abuse. But today, we wouldn't want it written any other way.

This story could not be written before now because the final chapter has just played out. We spent 20 years trying to bring glory to God for the work He was doing in our lives. But, in March 2007, we saw what God had been doing with and through us all those years, without our even knowing. It was extraordinary.

### Jeremy

As a young boy, I believed with all my heart that God would protect us and keep us safe if we would simply trust and obey Him. After our family was nearly destroyed while serving and obeying God on the mission field, I had a choice to make: Would I continue to believe in Him?

In my heart, I knew the only other option was to choose the enemy's side, and I would never do that. As I grew into a teen and then a young adult, I still believed in God, and even loved and did my best to obey Him. But I chose not to trust Him. After all, trust is earned, right? And to me, it seemed like God had failed that test.

Through the years, I have learned that my lack of trust was a result of my misconception of the character of God. In the pages of this book, you'll find my family's true story of healing, restoration and forgiveness. But you'll also find a testimony of renewed and increased trust in God the Father. I believe your life will be blessed as you read this book, and Father God Himself will reveal His deep love for you in a new and powerful way.

# INTRODUCTION

## Jadie

At 11 years of age, I never thought I would know hatred intimately.

After that fateful night in "paradise," not only did I know hatred; I also knew fear and lived it every day. Fear and hatred controlled my thoughts and actions.

I allowed the actions of someone else to control the very core of who I was, to completely change my personality and my character. What you perceive to be true, be it right or wrong, becomes your reality. That reality took me to a very dark place and many sleepless nights. I felt completely and utterly forsaken.

But in the depths of that darkness, I met Jesus. My encounter with Him changed my perception and changed my life. Understanding that I was not alone and that forgiveness was the key to my freedom gave me the courage to choose my own destiny.

I invite you to join my family and me in our real-life journey through the "valley of the shadow of death." In our narratives, you will find a common theme: God will never leave you nor forsake you! You will be challenged to step into God's perfect plan for you, no matter what life and the enemy have thrown your way.

Our story will lead you step by step to a life that goes beyond a tolerable recovery into an encounter with your Creator. So grab a box of Kleenex, and put on your hiking shoes. This is more than just a story; it's an adventure.

# Chapter One
# UNWELCOME STRANGER

**Darrell**

I do feel it. A darkness, a sort of heaviness in this place. I can't quite put my finger on it. When I see the bars on the windows and the heavy padlock on the sliding glass door, it's a sort of eerie reminder that danger lurked here once and could come again. *Safe.* It just doesn't feel safe. *Please, God, help me keep my family safe.*

**Sherri**

I could feel it, a subtle awareness that we were somehow unsafe. Shivering under the thin blanket, I glanced up at the barred windows above our bed. Outside, a soft breeze stirred through the palm trees as night descended. Off in the distance, I could hear the faint crashing of waves against rocks.

Our electricity had gone out hours ago. Now only the blackness of the night greeted us as we huddled together.

"Don't you and Jadie walk into the village alone," the former tenants had warned us. "It's not safe." I hadn't thought much of their words at the time. But now they echoed in my mind as I tossed and turned.

Outside our house, three large dogs paced the grounds, growling deeply every so often as though they, too, sensed something might not be right. The dogs had been left behind with the house, along with a well-used Toyota pickup truck and various appliances and furnishings.

I was not a particularly huge fan of dogs, but now, with a nagging feeling of uneasiness looming over me, I was thankful they were on the property. I shuddered and tried to close my eyes.

"Do you feel it, too?" I asked my husband, Darrell, nudging him gently. "A feeling that perhaps we aren't safe here?

We're so isolated, completely removed from the village. Remember what the former tenants told us about the break-ins they experienced?"

"Yes, I do remember. I feel it, too," Darrell agreed. "But we have to trust in the Lord. He's the one who has called us here to Palau. He will protect us."

I squeezed his hand gently. "You're right, of course," I agreed, thankful to have my husband by my side. I sighed and tried to get comfortable in our awkwardly shaped bed. (Another thing the previous tenants had left behind for us: an octagonal-shaped bed that was taking some getting used to!)

"I can't wait until the kids arrive. It's so difficult not having any communication with them. If something were to happen to them or us, we wouldn't even know how to get in touch."

"We have to just trust that the Lord has them in His hands, as He has us in His hands," Darrell whispered. "That's all we can do right now, Sherri. Pray and wait."

*Pray and wait.*

I closed my eyes and tried to ignore the noises outside that seemed to grow louder by the minute. By day, the tropical breeze that swept through the mangrove trees was enchanting. But at night, the wind set an eerie tone for the dark hours that lay ahead of us. I tried to shake off my anxiety, tried to remind myself that God was absolutely in control and would keep us safe no matter what came our way.

But after several nights of struggling with this unwelcome stranger known as fear, I cried out to God, "I can't live like this; I need Your help!" I opened my Bible and was directed to the book of Psalms, chapter 4. In reading through this short Psalm, I realized that verse 8 was the one I needed: "I will lie down and sleep in peace, for you alone, O Lord, make me dwell in safety."

Immediately I felt this promise giving me peace and from that moment on, I began sleeping better. After all, we were in a tropical paradise, a beautiful, picture-perfect island. What could possibly go wrong in paradise?

## Darrell

I felt the call to work in missions from a very early age. Raised in a Christian home in Forks, Washington, I accepted Christ as my Savior when I was just 8 years old. During a youth camp one summer, I felt the Lord calling me specifically into foreign missions, and I began to prepare for that direction in my life. Right after graduating from high school, I attended Northwest University, a Bible college located in Kirkland, Washington.

I met my beautiful wife, Sherri, there. Sherri had also felt the Lord calling her into missions when she was in her early teens. We were married at the end of our freshman year at the tender age of 18, both of us excited about living out the dream God had put into our hearts as children.

Two years after our wedding, Sherri gave birth to our son, Jeremy. Thirteen months later, his sister, Jennifer (who we would later nickname Jadie), arrived. Thus we accomplished an important piece of our life plan: to have our two children close together so they could be each other's best friend on the mission field. With our family complete, we were ready to forge ahead and do the work God had prepared for us.

Having spent all my life in Washington State, I was rather unsure of what to expect in a foreign country, but I knew that God would provide for us.

After spending a full year raising money for our future work on the mission field, God led our family to the Solomon Islands. We eagerly packed our belongings and flew across the Pacific, ready for whatever adventure He brought our way.

Guadalcanal was our first mission. Missionaries Ray and Becky Sparre met us at the airport. Tropical trees, coconut plantations and white sandy beaches greeted us. Our home was near Henderson Air Field, Red Beach and Iron Bottom Sound. These places all got their names during World War II. The island was teeming with history, which Jeremy and Jadie, now 10 and 9 years old, found especially fascinating.

We set about trying to connect with the islanders, who proved to be very warm and receptive. I quickly picked up Pidgin English, the national language. Though our surroundings were primitive, the children adjusted beautifully and soon Washington State began to feel light years away.

As we started the second year of our ministry, however, a feeling of unrest seemed to fall over the island. We soon learned that we were living smack dab in the middle of a culture only one generation out of cannibalism!

Though the islanders were generally harmless to outsiders, they often became violent among themselves.

We also found ourselves dealing with some moral issues within the local church leadership. Even though the activity in question was not culturally acceptable, they did not appreciate the white missionaries' leadership and subsequent actions.

One evening, a truckload of 12 formidable men from the church rumbled up to our house with a slew of machetes. They intended to attack Ray and me. Sherri and Becky instantly began calling on God for deliverance.

"This attack is not God's will," I told the would-be attackers as I silently prayed for divine intervention. After a long verbal exchange, the men backed down and left the premises.

We all rejoiced that God had heard and answered our prayers. "He is so faithful!" Sherri sobbed through her tears of thankfulness and relief. Together we praised God that He had intervened during what could have very well been the last moments of our lives.

Our mission's director, Wes Hurst, wept with us when he learned what had happened. He made a trip to the Solomons to meet with us and the church leadership. Following this meeting, a decision was made to remove the missionaries from the islands. "We'd like to transfer your family to the island nation of Palau. It's located in the mid-Pacific Ocean, just southeast of the Philippines. After what you have been through here, the ministry in Palau will be a piece of cake."

We prayed and agreed to go, grateful for the little time we had been able to spend in the Solomons and the impact we had been able to make on those we had met.

But Jeremy and Jadie were really saddened to leave the Solomon Islands. They had come to love the land and its people, as well as the rich history that surrounded us at every turn. Not wanting to put them through too much stress during our time of transition, Sherri and I decided it would be best to have the children return home to Washington for a few weeks while we settled into Palau.

After much conversation, we decided to allow them to travel unaccompanied to Fiji, on to Hawaii and then to Vancouver, B.C., where friends would meet them. We were relieved when we learned of their safe arrival.

Shortly before Sherri and I left the Solomons, she came to me, waving a letter she had just received in the mail. "Listen to this, Darrell! A lady named Jan wrote me. She said she saw my picture in a missionary magazine and felt led to write me. She said she has never written to someone she didn't know before, but that she was sure God wanted her to write me. She has been faithfully praying for our family ever since, and she just wanted to let me know. Isn't that incredible? And here's the fun part: She and her husband live in Hawaii and have invited us to visit them if we ever pass through there!"

"Awesome!" Darrell replied. "It's great to know we have people all over the world praying for us, even some we have never met. I bet they didn't expect for us to be passing through next week!"

A few days later, Sherri and I stopped in Hawaii on our way from the Solomon Islands to Palau and connected with

Jan and her husband, Jerry. They were wonderfully gracious and hospitable. We explained that our kids were visiting family in Washington State and would be joining us soon. Jerry was a travel broker and offered to assist with travel arrangements.

"I can't tell you how much this means to us," Sherri told Jan and Jerry repeatedly. "It will be difficult to be away from our children, but we know God has orchestrated all of these events, including all the help you have been to us. Thanks so much."

On our way to Palau, Sherri and I tried to gather all the information we could about the new place to which God was calling us. Nestled in Micronesia in the heart of the Pacific Ocean, Palau, we soon learned, was a tiny, independent nation of 12,000 people residing on a string of small islands. We would be going to the island of Babeldaub. Located in the western part of the country, Babeldaub is the largest island of Palau.

Our excitement mounted as we read about Palau's rich history and beautiful surroundings. "Listen to this, Sherri," I said eagerly, holding up an airline travel magazine. "It says here the island of Babeldaub is a high volcanic island of gently rolling hills, beautiful stretches of sandy beach on the east coast and mangrove forests on the west. There are more than 700 species of coral in the surrounding ocean, as well as 1,500 species of fish. Palau is also home to the world famous Rock Islands, which are comprised of emerald color limestone. Sounds picture perfect, doesn't it?"

"It does," Sherri agreed, leaning over my shoulder to examine a picture of the island. "A real tropical paradise, for sure."

When we were assigned to Palau, we learned that we would be taking over a house from a missionary family who had pioneered the work there and were now leaving the country. They would also leave behind for us a Toyota pickup truck, as well as some furnishings.

# UNWELCOME STRANGER

We would essentially be stepping right into their life as they stepped out. We were grateful and humbled to see how much God had already provided for us.

The moment the plane touched down in Palau, we began to pray. "God, whatever it takes to reach these people with the gospel, we are Your servants."

I was overtaken by the beauty of the place. I glanced over at Sherri, who was speechless as she surveyed the vast Philippine Sea, sparkling like a gem beneath the bright sunlight. "Pictures don't do this place justice," I whispered. "The Rock Islands are amazing. And did you see all the different shades of blue in the water? I can't wait to snorkel."

Our house, it turned out, was architecturally unique. It was built to maximize airflow. The lower floor had four octagon pods elevated on stilts and the second floor had one pod. The building's construction was wood frame with tin siding and roof. All the windows had bars covering them.

The building, overlooking the sea, sat secluded from the village of Ked (pronounced Keth). It was eight miles from Koror, the only city on the island. The house was both beautiful and formidable. "This thing looks pretty secure," Sherri remarked as she glanced at the heavy bars on the windows. Even the sliding door in the kitchen had bars and a heavy padlock.

"Remember what the former tenants said about the past break-ins," I reminded her. "I'm sure we'll be fine, though. This place is way out of the way." We stepped inside and surveyed the comfortable furnishings.

"Home sweet home," Sherri giggled.

We spent the next few days in our new residence struggling to meet our basic needs. We soon learned that the electricity only worked a few hours a day, forcing us to use a generator for our appliances.

Everything we relied on for comfort began to break down at once. The brand new television we had brought along so we could watch videos failed to work. The gas range refused to cooperate. Then, even the pickup truck began to fall apart. It didn't take us long to realize that Satan was launching a serious battle against us in our new place.

"I know this is a spiritual attack," I told Sherri one night as I struggled with one of the generators. I had spent all day trying to get the pickup truck working, only to come home to no electricity once again. Life was difficult, but we recognized our circumstances for what they were: Satan's scheme to bring discouragement.

"He certainly does try hard, doesn't he?" Sherri mused. "We won't let him beat us down, though. The Lord has called us here, and we will fulfill His purpose for us, even if we have to do it without electricity!"

Each day we sought to better prepare ourselves for the ministry to which God had called us. Sherri and I tried to familiarize ourselves with Palauan culture as much as possible. We had a strong desire to reach the youth of the island. The youth, we had learned, were well educated in American style schools but were often bored and frustrated because there were few jobs. We desired to reach them with the good news of Jesus Christ.

We also set out to secure a building for our ministry, but found it to be a much more difficult task than we had imagined. There were no Palauan believers in the church family at this time. We had been holding meetings near the Philippine labor housing area in a rickety, tin-covered chicken coop. It offered little shade, was hot and smelly and we had to deal with the occasional chickens and dogs. Finally, we were able to secure a meeting place in a small wood-framed building with a tin roof.

The former missionaries had built a puppet trailer that we pulled behind our Toyota pickup. Sherri and I visited many villages that were scattered around the island. The children loved the puppets and the Bible stories.

We were pleased to experience how gracious everyone was, but saddened that only the children took an interest in coming to hear the gospel.

Meanwhile, we had not heard a word from Jeremy and Jadie about when they would be arriving. We had no telephone in our house and were only able to call out from the island by making an appointment at a facility in town. Every time we heard a plane land, we drove down to the airport to see if our children had arrived. We waited until the very last passenger had debarked from the plane and then, disappointed, returned home.

"It's so hard not knowing when they are coming or where they are," Sherri said wistfully one night as we prepared for bed. It was almost 9 p.m., and the electricity was about to turn off, forcing us to head to bed early. "I just want to know they are safe and will be here soon."

"I know. It's so difficult being away from them. And I know they are so eager to come. I'm so proud of them. They have embraced our calling and have been such good sports throughout all of our adventures. I look forward to the time we are all together again and digging into the mission God has for us here."

That night, as I heard the dogs growl outside our house, I couldn't help but think about what Sherri had said. *Safe.*

Despite all the unrest on the Solomon Islands, we had rarely felt unsafe there.

But here, alone, in a house covered in bars and padlocks, I suddenly felt restless and apprehensive. I thought of the previous missionaries, who had relayed information to us about several acts of robbery that had taken place on these very premises — acts that had forced them to bar the windows. It seemed rather eerie that someone would seek out this place. It was so far from town. I tried to quiet my thoughts and turned to the Lord, asking Him to keep us secure and protected and to bring Jadie and Jeremy to us safe and sound, as well.

At last, the glorious day arrived when our children landed on the island. We greeted them with open arms and not a few tears. Jeremy appeared to have grown a few more inches, and Jadie was more beautiful than ever. While away from us, both had celebrated birthdays: Jeremy his 12th and Jadie her 11th.

One of our friends from the States had traveled with them, for which we were especially grateful. A wonderful tropical breeze whipped up around us as we drove home, eager to introduce our new surroundings to our kids.

"It's so warm," Jadie remarked as she stuck her head out the window.

"Don't forget how close we are to the equator," I reminded her. "Expect beautiful weather and warm rains while you're here. It's quite relaxing."

We passed through the village and pointed out a few things to the children. Cement blockhouses with tin roofs dotted the gravel and coral roads that weaved through the village. Children and teenagers were playing basketball and stopped as we passed, taking note of our kids.

I felt a sort of heaviness come upon me as I watched them and felt my heart break for the many here who did not know of God's great love for them. I could not wait to get Jeremy and Jadie involved with the children's ministry on the island. They were such naturals with other children.

"Wow, that house looks really weird," Jadie cried as we turned the corner and approached our home. "This is where we're going to live? Awesome!"

"Wait until you see the view," Sherri told her. "You'll be blown away."

As we pulled in the driveway, the picture postcard view greeted us: sparkling turquoise waters surrounding the famous Rock Islands and dancing palm trees. I wondered if I would ever tire of this amazing piece of scenery. "Thank You, God," I murmured. "What a wonderful Creator You are."

We made the decision to find someone to teach us the Palauan language. We had met a wonderful couple, Larry and Elena, who made us feel right at home on the island. Larry was American and Elena was Palauan. She was a local musician and agreed to teach us the language. She was so gifted and energetic that we often forgot she was blind! Larry was a judge and a wonderful person, as well.

"I'm so thankful we met Larry and Elena," Sherri told me one night after we tucked the children in. "They're such a wonderful Palauan influence and are so encouraging, as well. They certainly have helped this place feel more like home."

\*\*\*

On the morning of July 25, about nine weeks after we had arrived in Palau, Sherri and I awoke early, having tossed and turned all night thanks to having to share our octagonal-shaped bed with the children. A storm had rushed through during the night and, after lightning struck the house the second time, the kids decided to join us upstairs in our bed. But now the island seemed more peaceful and quiet than it had in days.

"What a beautiful morning," Sherri mused as she brewed some coffee. Thankfully, the electricity was on, and our appliances were cooperating.

"There's nothing like a morning after a storm," I replied.

We did our devotions and prayed together, thanking the Lord for a new, fresh day, and asking Him to bless it. The kids joined us as we prayed again, "God, whatever it takes to reach these people with the gospel, we are Your servants."

We were excited to embark on the first day of our "real life" as a new missionary family together in Palau. Our friend from back home had just left the night before, leaving the four of us together for the first time on the island.

When we finished breakfast, we piled into the pickup and headed down to Koror, the main town on the island. Though Koror was only eight miles away, the trip usually took closer to 30 minutes due to the winding gravel roads.

We traveled through our village of Ked and to the end of our island of Babeldaub. There we crossed the K-B Bridge (Koror-Babeldaub) and several causeways, which connected the tiny islands one to another.

"What's the plan today, Dad?" Jeremy asked as we rumbled down the gravel road.

"A ship just arrived yesterday, and we need to load up on groceries, stop by the bank and try to find some parts for that pesky generator," I replied. Going to town was always sort of an adventure, even if our objective was only to complete menial tasks.

Getting groceries on the island was no easy job. A ship carrying food and supplies arrived only once a month, and we wanted to get into town and obtain the freshest food we could possibly find. We were out of fresh food and also needed to restock the pantry with canned goods.

Upon arrival at the "island style" supermarket, we fanned out and quickly gathered the essentials: canned soup and vegetables, flour, sugar and some frozen meat. Fresh fruit and vegetables were a rare, welcome treat, and we knew we would pay dearly for them at the checkout.

While living in the Solomon Islands, we had grown accustomed to visiting the open market daily, where we could purchase all the fresh food we desired. But finding fresh food that was not spoiled or outdated was now a luxury. The hard red clay soil of Palau made gardening and growing vegetation very difficult. Therefore, Palauans came to rely on limited imports from the United States.

"I'm going to check on a part for the generator while we're here," I told Sherri as I hopped out of the pickup truck and headed for the hardware store. "If I can't fix it, it's going to be another long day without electricity."

It was difficult to keep the frozen foods from spoiling when the local electricity was off and the generator broke down.

"Another adventure!" Jeremy piped up.

# UNWELCOME STRANGER

I was so thankful the kids were flexible and settling in well to another new culture. They were a constant reminder to me to walk in faith, trusting that the Lord would indeed provide for all of our needs.

A few hours later, the truck rumbled up the hill across the K-B Bridge toward home carrying four happy but weary people and several sacks of precious groceries. It had been a long afternoon, but we were thankful for the time we had spent together.

"I know what we should do!" I shouted as we grabbed the groceries and headed for the house. "It's time to take those new motorcycles for a spin, don't you think?" We had recently replaced the motorcycles that we had left behind in the Solomons.

I didn't realize how fast my son could move as he dropped the groceries on the kitchen table and ran toward the garage. He was truly growing into a fine young man.

I raced after Jeremy, determined to prove that I could still out ride him, at least for now. I was so thankful to have had my children back for the past few weeks. Nothing brought me greater joy than spending time with them.

Sherri busied herself in the kitchen, preparing a special meal for us out of the produce and other food we had purchased in town. She peeked out the window several times to wave to us as we sped up and down the hill across from the house, showing off our skill to the village kids.

"This dinner is delicious, Mom," Jadie said quietly as she stabbed a piece of fresh fruit on her fork.

Sherri laughed. "Thank you, Jadie. I definitely am enjoying every bite after having gone without fresh fruit for a few weeks."

After dinner, the four of us settled down to watch a video on our newly repaired television. We knew we had just a couple of hours until the power went out again. Living on only three to five hours of electricity every day was a challenge, to say the least, but it forced us to become closer as a family; we had to become creative when the power went out.

I snuggled next to Sherri with the children at our feet, thankful once again for being reunited with my precious family. I didn't want to take a second with them for granted.

Our conditions may have been less than ideal at times, but at night, when the lights went out and we ended our day, I often felt like the richest man alive.

After the video was over, we settled the kids in their rooms and prayed with them. "Lord, thank You for a wonderful day. You have provided for us, and we are thankful for that. We pray You will keep us safe and give us the rest we need so that we can wake up and serve You another day."

As the kids drifted off to sleep, Sherri and I slipped out onto the deck and spent some quality time together as we swung in the hammock that I had just received for my 33rd birthday three days before.

Later, after we had quietly slipped upstairs and into bed, I lay back on the pillow and smiled. I thought about Jeremy and Jadie's squeals of delight as the motorcycles careened up and down the hill. I thought about Sherri, my beautiful bride, who was always so willing to accompany me on any adventure, so ready to love me and serve God. *A perfect day in paradise*, I concluded as I drifted off to sleep, the gentle ocean breeze rattling the palm trees just outside the house.

I had no hint of the nightmare that lay just ahead for us, a nightmare that, in only a few hours, would turn paradise into a living hell.

# Chapter Two
# ATTACKED

**Darrell**

Waking with a start in the middle of the night, I heard our three dogs barking frantically outside. Getting out of bed, I stumbled down the stairs. We had listened to a group of men partying on the hill above our house for a number of nights over the past few weeks, and I was certain they were up to mischief again.

"Quiet down, guys!" I called out to the dogs, cracking the back door open. Just then, a beer bottle flew out of nowhere and hit me squarely in the face. Stumbling back a moment from the shock and the pain, I peered out into the darkness to see where it had come from. I could hear voices approaching.

"Darrell, what's happening?" Sherri called from the top of the stairs.

I slammed the door and tried to bolt it. Moments later, more glass bottles began breaking against the bars on our windows. I quickly rushed Jeremy and Jadie upstairs just as Jadie's bedroom window shattered. My heart raced as I realized the men were going to try to make their way inside our home one way or another. I had to act quickly!

"Keep the kids upstairs!" I hollered up to Sherri, looking around for a makeshift weapon to protect my family. The previous missionaries had installed a battery-powered alarm on the house after a break-in. As I hit the panic button, a deafening sound echoed through the house. Surely, help would come soon! We were far from the village, but the sound was so loud that I knew someone would hear it.

Just then, two men broke through the front door — ripping it completely off its frame. The sound of wood cracking and splintering was nearly drowned out by the blaring alarm.

I grabbed a chair, hoping to block their entrance. But the men were already through the door and charged at me. Both men began throwing things at me. One hit me over the head with a piece of furniture. Still somewhat disoriented, I tried to get my bearings in the darkness. I stumbled back, scanning the room frantically for something else I could use as a weapon. I had to keep the men from reaching my family upstairs!

Before I could find anything, one of the men lunged at me, wielding a shotgun. He swung it around like a baseball bat. I caught a glimpse of the gun as it was in full swing. I tried to duck but not quickly enough. It caught me in the center of my forehead, knocking me back onto the kitchen floor. I reached up and felt blood trickling down my forehead.

A third man entered the house. They were all storming around, throwing things, cursing, yelling and demanding money. I thought quickly and grabbed for a folding chair from the dining room, holding it in front of me as a barrier. Blood was flowing freely from my head, and I knew I was hurt bad. Nevertheless, my adrenaline kicked in. Fighting my way down the hall, I backed up the stairs trying to stay between my family and the attackers. "Where's the money?" one of them demanded, the stench of his beer breath in my face.

I knew it was only a matter of time before they pushed past me and found my family in the bedroom at the top of the stairs.

I imagined how frightened they must be as they heard the commotion below.

*Please, God, protect them! Don't let them hurt my family!*

I had a dreadful feeling that these men were after more than money. They had obviously been drinking and were angrier than I'd ever seen anyone in my entire life.

These were not reasonable men who could be talked down with a few dollars and a calm word.

As the men pushed up the stairs, I yelled out, "Leave us alone! I'll get you what you want, just leave us alone!"

"Shut your face!" the man snarled. My head throbbed, and my side ached with each step. As they finally forced their way past me, I looked up and saw my precious wife as she sat on the bed holding Jeremy and Jadie, her eyes filled with terror. Matching terror filled their innocent eyes. *Oh, God, they don't need to see this! Let the men leave them alone!*

"Get on the floor!" I heard one of the men growl at Sherri and the children. The other men dragged me back downstairs and into the laundry room. One pointed a shotgun at my head and threatened to shoot me if I moved. I was so weak by this time that all I could do was pray. "Touch that door and you're dead, understand?" he yelled at me.

I slid down the wall and collapsed on the floor, all my strength gone. I tried to make out my surroundings in the darkness. Blood trickled down my head, the room began to spin and the nausea from the pain overwhelmed me. As a former Emergency Medical Technician, I knew I was in bad shape and that I could pass out at any minute. Praying silently, I willed myself to be strong; I had to stay conscious and calm for my family.

Time passed in what seemed like slow motion. Outside the room, I heard the terrified screams of my little girl and knew she was being abused by one or more of the men. *Oh, God, not my daughter! Not Jadie! She is just 11 years old, still a child!* "Leave her alone!" I shouted.

"Daddy …?" My sweet daughter's brave voice called from her room across the hall.

Once again, my heart broke as I realized my daughter's innocence was being robbed from her. If only there was something I could do! I felt myself go weak again and knew I must have lost a dangerous amount of blood from the attacks. *Please, God*, I began to pray silently, but my mind became a blur.

"Dad, I need your help!" Jeremy's panicked voice outside the door brought me back to my senses. "They want me to open the padlock on the garage door! Tell me where the keys are! Hurry!"

"They're in the kitchen on the counter," I replied frantically, sitting up straight and becoming instantly alert. *Oh, Jeremy!* I could tell he was trying to be brave, complying with the men's orders to avoid a horrible fate that could await him. Jeremy, just 12 years old, was trying to act like a man when I should be the one protecting him! My heart sank as I imagined the cruel mental games the men must be playing with him outside.

What could they possibly want in the garage? Whatever they were looking for, they were going to be disappointed. We were missionaries, not millionaires.

"Which key, Dad? What does the key look like?" One of the men thrust my son toward me into the laundry room. "I have one chance, or they're going to kill me," Jeremy mumbled. His attempt to be brave and calm only thinly disguised the panic in his voice.

"It's that one," I replied quickly, pointing to a certain key on the key chain. It was strange how details that had never mattered on a daily basis now suddenly became a matter of life and death.

*Trust in the Lord with all your heart, and lean not on your own understanding.* That Bible verse, one I had memorized as a child, suddenly came to my mind. It provided a moment of peace and comfort for me in my laundry room prison. *Lord, please, save us and rescue us from this nightmare. Please, God, help us!*

I was terrified, not for myself, but for my precious family. We had just barely settled into our new life together in Palau, and now our dreams and hopes were being shattered in an instant. We were being violated, invaded, attacked! Once again, I felt helpless and tried not to despair. Although we were being violently torn apart, I had to believe the Lord would watch over my family and somehow bring us out of this ordeal and back together again.

Again I heard the sounds coming from Jadie's bedroom, my heart breaking each time the noises echoed across the hall. I heard one of the men yelling at Jeremy outside and prayed he had been able to open the garage door. My thoughts shifted to Sherri, my precious wife. I had not heard her voice in a while. Where had they taken her? Had there been more men waiting for her outside? My heart broke for her. *Oh, dear God, please be with my wife, wherever she is! Let her be all right!*

I grabbed a damp towel from the laundry room floor and put it to my head. As the blood quickly soaked the towel, I realized once again how seriously I must be injured. I needed medical attention quickly, but somehow my injuries seemed insignificant compared to what my family was enduring.

At some point, I realized the man guarding me was gone. With all the strength I could gather, I stood, stepped into the hallway and called for my kids. I cringed as broken glass and wood cut my bare feet. I was weak and confused. But I needed to find my family.

**Sherri**

I awoke with a start when I heard the barking. Groggy, I sat up in bed and realized Darrell was shuffling downstairs to quiet the dogs.

Suddenly, I heard breaking glass and loud voices outside. I jumped out of bed and ran downstairs, calling out to Darrell, "What's happening?"

"Sherri, get the kids upstairs, now!" Darrell shouted. He slammed the back door just as I heard the horrible sound of glass breaking in Jadie's bedroom.

I quickly gathered Jeremy and Jadie and ran them upstairs, my heart pounding with every step I took. Suddenly, I was fully awake, and I knew something terrible was happening to us. We were being invaded. The safety of our home was shattered in a moment.

With the children sequestered upstairs in our bedroom, I crept to the edge of the stairs to see what was happening below. I heard Darrell trying to ward off the attackers, yelling at them to leave his family alone. Moments later, a deafening sound filled the walls of our house; the noise was so piercing I had to cover my ears. I soon realized it was the alarm the previous missionary tenants had installed. *Please, God, let someone hear the alarm and come to our rescue.*

The next few moments felt like hours as I heard the violent attack below, knowing Darrell was outnumbered and surely taking a horrific beating. Almost as if I was reliving a nightmare, the screams and the splintering sound of furniture breaking crashed through my mind. *Please, God, let someone come*, I prayed desperately. My heart beat wildly in my chest as I hovered at the top of the stairs, feeling helpless and afraid.

Suddenly, the alarm stopped, and I realized one of the intruders must have found it and smashed it. In the eerie silence, my heart sank. I realized to my horror that we were now prisoners in our own home, prey to the vicious men who had invaded it. My peaceful sleep had been transformed into a living nightmare.

Two men backed Darrell to the stairs, right into my view. I sucked in my breath as Darrell held a folding chair in front of him, trying to keep the men from coming upstairs. "Don't hurt my family!" he screamed at the men. "Don't hurt my family!"

"What do they want, Darrell?" I called out frantically. Perhaps we could give them what they had come looking for and they would leave!

"They want money," he replied feebly.

Another man appeared, and the three of them began to push Darrell up the stairs with force.

# ATTACKED

Jadie and Jeremy remained huddled on the bed at the top of the stairs, their terror reflected in their eyes. *Please, God, not my children! Let them leave my children alone!*

"Where's the money?" the men demanded, their voices growing angrier with each forceful step they took. They kicked and hit Darrell from the right and the left.

"I already told you, we don't …" Darrell began, but before he could finish speaking, the man hit and kicked him again, launching him onto the floor with such force that I had to look away.

"Shut your face!" the men screamed, continuing their abuse just inches from my feet. Their voices were merciless, animal like, and full of pure rage.

Darrell struggled to find his wallet while the men continued to kick and hurl punches at him. Suddenly, one of the men kicked me in my side and in my head.

"Get on the floor, all of you!" they screamed. "Now!"

As the children and I fearfully complied, one of the men grabbed Darrell and dragged him downstairs. I heard him threaten my husband as he shoved him into the laundry room below.

"Touch that door and you're dead, understand?" came the threat from below.

"All right, we'll try you. Where's the money?" One of the men shone a flashlight directly at me, and for the first time, I saw his horrible, raging eyes up close.

I cowered and shook my head. "We don't keep money in the house," I replied, willing my voice to stay calm. My answer obviously upset him. He kicked me to the floor and hit me, then pulled my head up by my hair and kicked me to the floor again. Downstairs, I heard Darrell yelling at the men, insisting they leave his family alone. *Oh, Darrell!* My heart went out to my husband, knowing he was fighting bravely for us with all the strength he could muster. Moments later, I heard a loud smack, and then silence. *Oh, dear God, what did they do to him? What did they do to my husband? Is he still alive?*

Two of the men inched toward me and began to pull at my clothes and touch me. I realized what they intended to do, and my heart stopped in my chest. "Please! Not in front of my children!" I pleaded. I could not bear for my children to witness such horror.

One of the men, who I guessed to be taking orders from the other, pushed me toward the stairs and through the house. In the darkness, I tripped over several pieces of splintered furniture. I realized, for the first time, what terrible damage had taken place downstairs. I felt sickened as I thought about the fight Darrell had tried to put up in order to protect his family.

"Leave them alone!" I heard Darrell holler from the laundry room. The third man stood guard in front of the laundry room door. My husband was alive, thank the Lord! Still, I knew he must be badly hurt and desperate to protect us.

We arrived at the front door, and I realized it had been completely broken off its hinges. There was a two- to three-foot drop to the ground. The man pushed me outside, and I fell to the ground, tears filling my eyes as I landed on the cold, hard surface.

As the man blindfolded me, fear rose in my chest as darkness covered my eyes. Suddenly, I became very disoriented. The man marched me away from the house, the gravel crunching beneath my bare feet. I felt as though we walked for miles, but it could have really been just a few yards. I had no idea. I had become nothing more than a puppet.

The man stopped me suddenly, pushed me to the ground and began to sexually abuse me. I cringed, turning my head away from the stench of his beer breath. I prayed the whole thing would end quickly.

When he was finished, he pulled me to my feet and walked me back to the house. I shuddered as the chill of the night pricked my skin. I had already endured so much; surely he would leave me alone now!

We reached the yard and, to my horror, I heard the small voice of my precious daughter crying. *Oh, dear God, they're hurting Jadie! They're hurting my sweet little girl!* My heart broke for my daughter, whose virginity and innocence had been robbed of her in the most horrid of ways. *Please, let them leave her alone!*

"Take me instead! Leave her alone and take me!" I cried out, hoping her attacker would hear me, wherever he was.

"Where is the money? Tell me!" I heard another man nearby demand.

"We don't have any," came the surprisingly calm voice of my son.

Tears filled my eyes behind the thick cloth of my makeshift blindfold. I simply felt I could not go on anymore. The horrific events of the night suddenly caught up with me, and I felt weak and despondent.

*God, where are You? Where are You in this?*

I felt that He had truly abandoned us at that moment, and a piece of my heart began to die. We had come to Palau to serve God and instead had faced one trial after another. The unfaithful generator and broken-down truck had been frustrating, but nothing compared to this! *Oh, God, where are You? Where are You?*

At that very moment, God spoke gently to my heart. He reminded me of a lesson I had heard at our School of Missions a few years before. A man by the name of Charles Greenaway had spoken on the subject of suffering and sacrifice. He told the story of three Hebrew men, Shadrach, Meshach and Abednego, recounted in Daniel, chapter 3.

The men were condemned to a fiery furnace after refusing to bow down to the golden image King Nebuchadnezzar had set up. They spoke these very powerful and profound words at that pivotal moment:

"Our God whom we serve is able to deliver us from the burning fiery furnace, and He will deliver us from your hand, O king. **But if not**, let it be known to you, O King, that we do not serve your gods or worship the golden image which you have set up."

Those words penetrated my heart in that very moment when I felt I simply could endure no more. I clearly heard God speak these words to me: "Sherri, this is your 'if not.' Choose whom you will serve."

In that moment, I felt a fire in the depths of my soul. I realized that my God truly did care about the very treacherous circumstances of my life. I knew that my only hope of survival was to trust in Him. I heard the Lord say, "Sherri, you will not die tonight."

"Come on," came a gruff voice beside me, jolting me from my thoughts. Another man was now walking me away from the house in a different direction. My heart thumped in my chest again, knowing the torture was far from over.

"I'm going to take you as my prisoner forever and keep you captive and abuse you for the rest of your life," the man whispered in my ear, cackling. "Your precious little husband will be killed, as well as your children. You'll be left alone in this country as my private possession." He cackled again, an evil cackle that sent shivers up my spine.

I remembered the Lord's words, which had come just when I feared my heart could endure no more. He had promised that I would not die tonight! But in this moment of darkness, I did not find comfort in those words.

Still blindfolded, I heard a large steel door being opened in front of me and felt myself being thrust down into the rocky dirt. I had no idea where we were, but would later learn we were inside an old World War II weapons bunker.

"Why did you come here, you stupid, rich Americans?" the man asked, his slurred voice angry and bitter.

"We came here to share the gospel of Jesus Christ with the people of Palau," I replied, trying to keep calm.

# ATTACKED

"We believe that God so loved the world that He sent His only Son, Jesus, to die for our sins, so that we might go to heaven to be with Him and not perish in hell." I was surprised at how easily the words fell off my tongue. I knew that, despite my torture, I had to share the good news of Jesus with this man.

"Jesus, huh?" To my surprise, the man listened to my words.

"Yes. He loves us all so much. It breaks His heart to see us sin. But the good news is we can be forgiven for even the worst of sins. He is so merciful, so good."

Tears filled my eyes as I spoke the words.

The man continued to listen, but then began to sexually abuse me again. I clenched my fists and closed my eyes, trying to put myself anywhere but this horrible place. Once again, God spoke to my heart, reminding me that I would not die in this place. This time, His words brought great comfort to my soul. My God had not abandoned me, even though I had literally hit rock bottom.

The hours passed with little reprieve. I slowly began to realize that I was being bitten by an army of insects.

I thought of Darrell and the children and how brave they had all tried to be back at the house. Were they still alive? *Oh, God, please let them still be alive!* The thought of being the sole survivor of this nightmare was nearly too much for me to bear. I cried out to God in my heart, asking Him once again to deliver us all. I was beginning to feel weak and sleepy and fought to stay awake.

## Darrell

I may have passed out at some point, as the night became a blur of darkness and terrible noises. After what seemed like an eternity, Jeremy and Jadie were at my side. We nearly smothered each other as we embraced with relief.

"I'm sorry, I'm so sorry," I muttered, clutching onto my precious kids. I knew they had endured the very horrors I had vowed to protect them from. That thought broke what was left of my heart. But somehow holding them then gave me the peace and the strength to move on. "We need to go for help. I don't know where your mom is, but I have to believe she is alive. We're safer leaving this place than we are staying here."

"Dad, your head," Jeremy began, inspecting my skull cautiously. "It's bad, Dad. There's blood everywhere."

"I'm going to be okay," I replied, trying to be strong for my children. Jadie and Jeremy looked up at me with terrified but trusting eyes.

Again I closed my eyes and gathered my strength, this time for the climb up the stairs. I quickly found a flashlight, pulled on a t-shirt and a pair of gym shorts, then stumbled back down the stairs. "Keys! We have to find the keys to the truck, kids!"

Water was running in the house. The entire floor was wet. It appeared the men had dragged a garden hose into the house in an attempt to flood it. To the left and the right of me, heaps of furniture lay in pieces, a reminder of the vicious attacks that had taken place just hours before. With the curtains pulled to the ground and the doors and walls knocked in, the house resembled a war zone. I shuddered and tried to stay focused on the mission: find the truck keys and get out of here to find help as quickly as possible.

At last, we found the keys. The kids helped me out of the house and into the pickup. I figured it must be between 4 and 5 in the morning. I had to get help … fast! I called out for Sherri several times with no response. I then made the most difficult decision of my life — to leave her behind and go for help.

"Please start," I muttered as I turned the keys in the ignition of the little pickup truck. To my relief, it sputtered to life, and Jeremy, Jadie and I rumbled down the road. Jeremy sat next to me in case he had to drive. I was not sure I could stay conscious.

# ATTACKED

We pulled into several driveways in the village honking the horn and trying to get somebody's attention. We stopped at three houses with no luck.

"We'll go to the Seabee camp, it's not far and they will help us," I told the kids. I put my hand to my head for a moment, thankful I did not have a mirror in front of me to see the damage that had been done.

"You're hurt bad, Daddy," Jadie said softly, looking up at me with sad eyes.

"I know, honey, I know. We're gonna make it." I was amazed that I had the strength to drive in my condition.

## Sherri

The hours and minutes continued to blur together in the darkness. Suddenly, I heard noises outside the heavy metal door. The voices were speaking in Palauan. More attackers?! Fear gripped me as the men's voices grew closer and closer.

Then the man pushed my face to the ground. "Shut up!" he hissed at me and stood to see what was going on outside. He pushed open the door and ran into the darkness.

I heard movement and a scuffle outside the door, as though many men had come to the site. Once again, fear overwhelmed me like never before. I was sick at the thought of this nightmare continuing a moment longer.

"Mrs. Beebe, come out. It's okay. We're here to help you." His kind words were the sweetest sounds I'd ever heard. They were rescuers, not attackers!

My God had delivered me. I was going to be okay!

Slowly I stood, brushing insects and dirt from my body. With shaking legs, I stumbled out of the cave. One of the men quickly came to my side and offered me his jacket. I accepted it gratefully.

"Your family is alive," he told me. "They are at the Seabee camp. Come with us, and we will take you to them."

My family was alive! My heart sang. My family was alive! *Oh, God, thank You! Thank You!*

Suddenly, nothing else mattered; my family was alive, and we would soon be reunited!

The men led me back to the house just as dawn began to break. One of them handed me his flashlight. "We'll wait right here for you while you gather what you need. It's safe in there now, we promise," he told me gently.

I nodded and gingerly stepped over the threshold and into the house, ready to face the aftermath of the events. But nothing could have prepared me for the horrible scene that lay before me.

Broken furniture was strewn everywhere, holes were punched into the walls, curtains were pulled down off of the windows and water covered the floor. It truly looked like a scene out of a horror movie. I was saddened, not because our material possessions had been destroyed, but because the wreckage represented the awful abuse my entire family had endured.

Trembling, I retreated up the stairs to my bedroom. As I climbed the stairs, my mind was flooded with the horror-filled images from the night. My heart sank when I saw the once white bedspread now stained with the blood of my loved ones.

I rummaged through my belongings in search of something to wear. I pulled on the first thing I could find and stumbled back downstairs again.

It was then I noticed the blood everywhere: on the walls, on the handrails, on the furniture. I could not imagine what my poor family had endured during the hours we had been separated. I sloshed through the water that now stood two inches deep throughout the house and retreated outside, away from the gruesome sight.

Outside, the dogs greeted me, eagerly licking my hands. One of the dogs, Lucy, had been badly beaten.

I patted her awkwardly on the head, tears filling my eyes as I realized that even the dogs had endured terrible abuse. Lucy died later that day from the beating.

# ATTACKED

To the left of me, I saw a handcuffed man lying face down on the grass. I knew it was my attacker and quickly looked away. I was so thankful he had been caught and that he would be able to abuse me no longer.

"We're going to take you to your family now," one of the rescuers told me gently. He and the other men had gone out of their way to treat me with respect and care, for which I was so grateful. I was sure they knew I had endured the worst kind of abuse.

The men led me into a tiny, beat up foreign car. I climbed awkwardly into the back and sunk into the seat, breathing a much overdue sigh of relief. As we began to drive down the road, a song swelled in my heart. I could not resist the urge to sing it out loud:

> "In moments like these, I sing out a song
> I sing out a love song to Jesus.
> In moments like these, I lift up my hands
> I lift up my hands to the Lord.
> Singing I love you, Lord
> Singing I love you, Lord
> I love you, Lord."

I realized at that moment that my poor escorts in the front seat must have thought I had lost every bit of my senses. Feeling overwhelmed with gratitude to the Lord, I could not resist singing another song that came to my heart:

> "I love you, Lord
> And I lift my voice
> To worship you
> Oh my soul, rejoice
> Take joy my king
> In what you hear
> Let it be a sweet, sweet sound
> In your ear."

## Jeremy

Outside, I heard dogs barking and glass breaking against the bars on the windows. What was going on? The next thing I knew, Dad and Mom were telling me and Jadie to get upstairs quickly.

"What's going on, Mom?" I whispered. "It sounds like someone is trying to break in." My first instinct was to jump up and help my dad.

"Dad is checking on the noises. He told us to wait upstairs," Mom replied.

"Get out of here!" I heard my father shout downstairs. *Oh, please, God, keep my father safe!* I prayed. I heard a loud banging below, as though someone was trying to break in the front door. Suddenly, I heard yelling. The voices did not belong to my father. They were loud, angry and perhaps drunken. More banging followed, and once again, I heard my father's desperate plea to leave us alone.

"Get out of here! Leave my family alone!" I heard my father yell. I cringed. We were being invaded! What would someone want with us? We didn't have anything valuable. Why were they here? I didn't feel quite so brave anymore. I wanted my father to protect us, to fight off the bad men and scare them away.

The next few moments were like a scene out of a horror movie. Three men pushed my dad up the stairs where my mother, sister and I sat huddled on the bed. Though it was nearly pitch black, I could make out their formidable silhouettes. Their footsteps were loud and angry, their voices callous.

"Where's the money?" one of the men growled, hitting my dad and knocking him to the floor. One man dragged him back downstairs. Another man yanked my mom from my side. "Tell me where the money is, you stupid American!"

"We don't have any money," my mother pleaded, her voice desperate. I heard her whimper softly as the man hit her and threw her to the floor. How could this be happening? This was too awful to be real!

"No! Not in front of my children!" my mother screamed, as the man tore at her clothes.

I lowered my head and covered my eyes, knowing the man was about to do something terrible to my mom.

All of a sudden, they pulled Mom to her feet and took her downstairs. I was shaking all over and praying they would leave us all alone. Where was my father? Was he badly hurt? I no longer heard him struggling downstairs.

"You're comin' with me, boy." Another man appeared by my side and pushed me forcefully down the stairs.

Though terror ran through my veins, I did not dare put up a fight. I did not want to die.

The unknown loomed before me, a stretch of dark and horrible possibilities. *Please, God, don't let them hurt my family! Let them leave us alone!* I fought back tears, knowing they would do no good.

A cool breeze suddenly encompassed me, and I realized we were now outside. I heard the crunch of gravel beneath the man's feet as he shoved me along. He stopped after several steps, and I realized we were in front of the garage. I felt something cold against my forehead and gulped hard. A gun! He was holding a pistol to my head! These things only happened in movies, not to Jeremy Beebe, a missionary's kid!

"Open the padlock, kid," the man growled, nudging the gun against my temple. I knew that with just one click, he could end my life. I had to think fast.

"I don't know where the key is," I replied meekly, hoping my voice did not sound as small as I felt.

"Find it!" the man cried angrily. I could smell beer on his breath only inches from my face.

"Where is my father? He knows where the key is," I tried to reply calmly. My young body shook beneath his grip. I kept thinking about the gun pointed at my head and how I stood at his mercy, a click away from death.

"Then ask him!" the man growled, dragging me back inside. He thrust me into the entrance of the laundry room, where I saw my father only half-conscious in the corner.

Relief flooded me as I realized he was alive, but one look at him was all it took for me to also realize he was badly hurt. In the darkness, I could make out blood trickling down his face. Dad held his head and looked at me, distraught.

"Dad, I need to know where the key is for the padlock on the garage," I pleaded, hoping my voice did not sound as panicked as I felt. "I have one chance or they're going to kill me."

He looked up weakly and spoke. "I think they are in the kitchen on the counter," my father replied. I quickly retrieved them and ran back to Dad, holding up the keys. "This is the one," he added, pointing to a certain key dangling from the key chain.

"Are you sure?" I asked, my eyes pleading.

My father nodded. "I think so, son. I think so." His eyes had fear written all over them. We weren't just talking about keys, but about life and death!

The man kept the gun to my head as he pushed me across the room, back outside into the dark. "Now open it!" he growled. "Hurry up!"

My fingers shook so violently I nearly dropped the keys as I tried to fit the right one into the padlock. *Come on, come on!* I had heard people talk about dreams where they tried to dial the phone or open a door but remained frozen in motion. I felt like that. My heart raced as I tried the key. *Please, please work!*

"Hurry up! What's the problem?" the man sneered, his voice growing angrier by the minute.

"I'm trying," I whimpered, wishing my fingers would stop shaking so badly.

"Make it fast. This game is getting old," the man retorted, bearing his cold, rough fingers down around my neck. "You don't get that lock open, I shoot. Understand?"

# ATTACKED

"Yes," I whispered, fighting back tears. I knew he meant business. I had to turn that key!

To my utter relief, the lock sprang open, and I yanked the padlock off the door. "All yours," I told the man victoriously. In case my father could hear, I called out, "I got it, Dad!"

"Good job, son!" my father called out from inside the laundry room, as though we were playing a fun game of hide and seek. We both knew this was no time for fun and games, though. Our lives were at stake.

"Move outta' my way," the man growled. He pushed me aside and opened the garage door. Inside, I heard him pushing things around angrily. I wondered what he could possibly be looking for. We didn't own anything valuable. Why was he so insistent on looking through the garage?

I sat crouched on the gravel, shivering. It seemed the temperature had dropped drastically in the past few minutes. I thought I heard a girl scream in the background, and I cringed. Jadie! I prayed the men weren't hurting her, wherever they had taken her. And Mom, where was my mom? My head spun as I thought about my family, snatched from me in just a few horrible moments. Would I ever see them again?

"I'm not done with you, kid," the man snarled, grabbing me by the arm with such force I feared he might jerk my arm out of the socket. He yanked me back into the house and into the kitchen, where he began pulling kitchen drawers out one by one. I assumed he was still looking for money and knew he would not find any there. He grew angrier and angrier by the moment as he rummaged through drawer after drawer, cupboard after cupboard. "Stupid Americans!" he growled, obviously disappointed.

I did not dare ask questions as he pulled me back through the house and out onto the back deck and threatened to throw me off the edge and shoot me as I fell. Just yesterday, my father and I had raced our motorcycles past this very spot, watching the sun set against the beautiful ocean.

Now that peaceful memory seemed a lifetime away. I had been thrust into the middle of a nightmare.

"I'm gonna throw you off the side of this cliff here, boy, and there's lots of crocodiles down there. They'll devour you in no time, rip the limbs off your body and tear you apart till you're nothing but blood and bones." He cackled an evil laugh. "How do you like the sound of that?"

I knew this ledge very well and knew there was a good chance I would survive if he threw me down it. It was steep, but not deathly steep. I could most likely escape with a few cuts and bruises and make my way back up the hill if he threw me down. The practical side of me tried to plot my escape as he held me inches from the edge. I was not going to die! I was only 12 years old, and I was not ready to die!

"Heard of a little game called Russian Roulette, boy?" the man asked, his voice taunting. "Goes something like this. I spin the cylinder and pull the trigger. And then, maybe, you die. Ha-ha!"

I knew very well what Russian Roulette was, and I didn't like the sound of it one bit. I hated that gun and wished it would drop out of his hands and fall down the cliff. I knew better than to put up a struggle, though. *God, help me!* I prayed instead. *Please, save me! Don't let this man kill me out here!*

The man gripped me tightly with one hand and spun the cylinder with his other. He then put it to my temple, and I heard a dreaded click. Half expecting a loud explosion, I was relieved when nothing happened. "Stupid thing!" the man growled, slamming the gun against his thigh. He spun it again and shoved it back against my temple.

My heart stopped, and I sucked in my breath. *No, please don't go off! Let it be empty!*

To my utter relief, the gun clicked again, and again, nothing happened.

"Stupid gun!" The man threw the gun to the ground and slapped me, as though it were my fault it was not working. I knew he was angry that his little game had not worked as he had planned. He hit me again.

I winced in pain, but thanked the Lord that he had not shot me. Was the gun really empty, or had God allowed it to not work? Either way, I was more than relieved to be alive. I only prayed God had spared the lives of my family, as well.

"Come on, kid!" The man dragged me back across the deck and into the house, where he thrust me into the laundry room with my dad. "You're good for nothin'!" he growled, kicking me once more like a used tin can. He turned and stormed out of the house.

I scooted toward my father as the adrenaline drained from my body. He pulled me close to him with all the energy he could muster. "Are you all right, Jeremy?" he whispered weakly. "I'm so sorry, son. Are you okay?"

I shook my head bravely. "I think so, Dad. I'm okay. He tried to play Russian Roulette with me, but the gun wouldn't go off. He was getting really mad." I shuddered as I realized once again how truly close I had come to death. We moved into the hallway where there was some moonlight.

"Thank God it didn't," my father replied, shaking his head. He looked me up and down. "Are you sure you're okay?" Then Dad wrapped his arms around me. Neither of us could find words, but I knew he was telling me we were going to make it.

"I'm okay. But, Dad, your head, there's blood everywhere." I was used to seeing my father brave and strong, and it pained me to see blood dripping down his face and onto his chest.

"What does my head look like, Jeremy? They banged me up pretty good," my father said slowly.

I took a close look and winced at what I saw. My father's head was indeed "banged up pretty good." There was a big dent in his head, and it was still bleeding. I had never seen anything like it aside from my science book.

"It looks pretty bad, Dad," I replied quietly. "I think your skull is cracked." I felt sick as the words came out of my mouth.

My father nodded. "Lucky I have a hard head," he said quietly.

Just then I heard a quiet voice calling, "Dad … Jeremy … Mom …" It was Jadie, my little sister! *Oh, God, let her be okay*, I prayed. What had she endured? She was just a little kid!

"Dad, it's Jadie." Dad opened his arms and the three of us embraced, crying tears of relief.

"I'm so sorry, so sorry, honey," my father muttered, stroking my sister's hair as she trembled in his arms.

"Where's Mom?" I whispered, trying not to cry. Suddenly, the events of the night were starting to catch up with me. At first, it had just been a bad dream, but now, with Jadie back with us, it began to feel horribly real.

I wanted to wake up, to pinch myself right out of this nightmare and back into the safety of my own bedroom.

"I don't know, son," my father replied, his voice sad and dejected. "I have to believe she is alive, though. I just have to."

"We're going to go for help," my father insisted. "I know I'm hurt, but I'm pretty sure I can drive. We just have to find the keys to the truck and get out of here. I hate to leave without your mom, but it isn't safe here. I don't know if the men are still on the property or not."

We found the keys and started for the truck. Dad took a few steps and needed my help. My strong dad, my hero, was now leaning on me for support.

I knew he was operating on fumes of adrenaline, as he was obviously terribly wounded. Could he really drive us to safety in his condition? And would we really find help? Would we ever find Mom?

"Why is there water running?" I asked.

# ATTACKED

"I think they tried to hose the place out," my father replied. "Maybe they were trying to cover up evidence. They must have seen it in a movie or something."

A movie. That's all this was. It wasn't a bad dream, it was a movie, the kind I was not allowed to watch because I was only 12 years old.

Only I knew better. It was no movie, and I was not watching television. It was happening to me, a real live nightmare. Just a couple hours before, I had been curled up quietly asleep in my warm bed.

And now I was here, helping my bleeding father and my sister as we headed for the pickup. We had to find help. How could this be happening? Suddenly, home seemed millions of miles away as we drove down a dark, bumpy road in a country not our own.

## Jadie

I awoke in the middle of the night to the sound of the dogs barking outside. Rubbing my eyes, I sat up in bed and heard the frightening sound of glass breaking. Disoriented and afraid, I stumbled out of bed to the doorway. My dad was directly in front of me at the back door.

Dad turned and yelled at Jeremy and me, "Get upstairs with Mom!" I could hear more glass breaking, dogs barking and a terrible commotion outside. What on earth was going on? Was I having some sort of bad dream?

Terrified, I began to move in slow motion. I watched as Dad slammed the back door shut as beer bottles broke against it. "Get out of here!" he yelled at the men outside, trying to ward off whoever was on the other side of the door. Pushing us toward the stairs, he ran for the kitchen in search of something to protect us, while I stumbled up the stairs with Jeremy.

I began to shake uncontrollably as Jeremy crouched beside me, equally terrified. Then, in a matter of seconds, I heard the men breaking through the front door into the living room.

"Daddy," I whimpered, tears springing to my eyes.

There was lots of noise, and then the alarm went off. Talk about loud. "Leave my family alone!" my father yelled. Though we could not see anything, we heard a loud fight and knew my father must be badly hurt. How could this be happening to my family? Just moments before, we were just a missionary family living the dream God had called us to. Now, we were victims of a violent crime, helpless and unprepared to protect ourselves from this deadly attack.

The men hurled up the stairs toward us in a rage. At the first glimpse of the men coming toward us, my blood seemed to turn to ice in my veins. I trembled in fear and huddled closer to my brother and my mom, desperate to find safety between them. I prayed they would leave us alone. Why would they want to hurt us? What had we done to them?

I could feel my mom trembling next to me, but her head was high and her shoulders set as she stepped between us as the men headed toward us. Two men grabbed at her and began roughing her up, while my brother and I watched helplessly. "Where's the money? Give us the money!" they screamed.

"We don't have any money," my mother replied, her voice distraught. "Please leave us alone! Please don't hurt my children!"

The men ignored her cries and began to tear at her clothes. The sight was nearly too much for me. My mom, my best friend, being touched by such evil men. My mind struggled to process the scene playing out before me as I was taking in the images I had been protected from all my life ... until now.

"Not in front of my children!" my mother pleaded. "Please, not in front of my children!" *Please don't hurt her!* I wanted to yell out, but the words remained frozen on my tongue. This simply could not be happening to us!

# ATTACKED

Then, the men abruptly yanked my mom down the stairs and took her away. *No, no, no!* Where were they taking her? Would they hurt her? Kill her? Would we be next? My body shook as I held back quiet sobs. I caught Jeremy's eye, and we exchanged a glance that assured me we were feeling the same empty hopelessness. The sinking realization came over me that we were now alone and without our parents' protection for the first time in our lives. It was at that moment I knew we were far from invincible, and these unwanted guests were not planning to leave. Would I ever see Mom again? I could not bear the thought of anything happening to either of my parents, or my brother. We were all so close. Just last night we had been swinging happily in the hammock together as the sun went down, and now we were unwillingly thrown into circumstances far beyond the worst nightmare my 11-year-old mind could fathom!

One of the men yanked my brother away from the place where he huddled next to me. Before I knew what was happening, the other man had pulled me down the stairs. My little legs struggled to keep up with him as he dragged me across the room. I could hardly see a thing inside the pitch-black house, but I knew wherever he was taking me could not be good. I had never been so terrified in my entire life.

"Shut up, little girl, you're all mine now!" The man shoved me onto my bed and proceeded to rape me while I lay there trying to understand what was happening to me. So quickly, my innocence turned to awareness, and my fear turned to an anger I had never felt before. *Please, Daddy, come rescue me! Help me!* Again, the words remained frozen on the edge of my tongue. I bit my tongue hard and forced back the tears, trying to distance myself from the pain in my body.

"Don't hurt her." I heard my dad's pleading voice coming from the laundry room nearby. My dad was alive!

I was comforted to hear his voice and to know he was alive, but as the sounds of that terrifying fight echoed in my ears, I wondered how long he could hold on. *Let it be over soon! Let this nightmare be over!*

A million thoughts flooded my mind as the horror continued. Where had they taken my mom? And Jeremy? Were they alive? I tried to think of them, of my dad, of anything but the horrible place I was in as the man took advantage of me. I had never even smelled alcohol, but I knew enough right now to know I hated it more than anything. The man reeked of it, and I choked back the taste of vomit.

A second man entered my bedroom, and I knew that horror movie I just experienced was about to be replayed, and as the main character, I had no choice but to participate. I blinked my eyes open, taking in the silhouette of his scary face. Both men looked like monsters to me — horrible, terrible monsters who belonged only in bad dreams. "What do I do with her now?" the one man growled when it was over.

The men threw me into the laundry room across from my bedroom, where my father lay on the cold floor, covered in blood. I gasped at the sight of him, his face so swollen and stained with blood it was hardly recognizable. I crawled over next to him and began to sob, while he pulled me toward him with what little strength he had.

"Where is Jeremy?" I whispered, fearing the worst for my brother. "And Mom? Where did those bad men take her?"

My father shook his head and looked at me with sad, hollow eyes. "I don't know, honey. I'm so sorry. So sorry. Oh, dear God, we ask You right now to comfort us, to heal us and to protect us. Please, Lord, don't let them harm us anymore."

*Daddy, make it stop!* my heart cried silently as I melted into him, finding so much comfort in his arms. We were both quiet as we strained to hear a familiar voice in the night, hoping against hope that Mom and Jeremy were still alive.

A flashlight lit the room, and another man came at me. He grabbed my arm and tore me away from my father and down the hall. I was beyond terrified. I had thought the nightmare was over, but now it seemed it was anything but.

He scooped me up into his arms and carried me out of the house the same way Dad would have. The comparison between my father and this rapist repulsed me. Just moments before, I was in the safety of my daddy's arms, and now I was being carried away by a man that would surely fill my nightmares the rest of my days.

Throwing me to the ground like a rag doll, he hissed, "Now listen here. You'll do as I say, understand? I'm going to take you to my house, and you're never going back. You're going to remain my prisoner forever. You can forget your family. We will kill them all. So you best do what I say, or you'll be next, got it?" With my innocence now gone, the awareness of what was to come again washed over me, and I felt the devastation settle in. I felt myself losing the will to live. *Please, God, let him not be right! Let my family be alive!* I prayed.

I don't remember the next few moments, but somehow, I managed to break free of the man's drunken grip. I walked back to the house like a zombie. Stepping carefully, I entered the hallway. I needed to see if my father was alive. Soft sobs wracked my body as I made my way toward the laundry room, fearing the worst.

To my relief, my father was in the hall. I was so thankful that he was alive. I could see blood on Dad's head as he made his way toward me for a weak hug.

"Jadie, you're alive! I was so afraid they weren't going to let you go. I don't know where Mom is." His voice cracked at the mention of her.

As my thoughts went to Mom, knowing what I had endured the last few hours, a scream caught in my throat, and I was overwhelmingly aware of the danger she was still in. Then I saw Jeremy standing there, his eyes filled with sadness. I could not even imagine the nightmare he had gone through while we were apart.

"We have to get out of here and go for help," my father whispered, pulling us toward him.

"I need to put some clothes on," I murmured.

"Do it quickly while we try to find the truck keys."

"You're hurt, though, Dad. Can you drive?" I whispered.

"I'll have to. We have no choice."

I knew he was trying to be calm and brave for Jeremy and me. I stumbled into my bedroom and pulled on a sweatshirt and overalls. Then, on a whim, I added a second layer of clothing. Somehow, I just knew Mom was alive. The man had lied about killing Dad and Jeremy, and I was sure that somewhere, my mom was still alive. No doubt she would need clothes when we found her, I reasoned. As the thought flooded through my mind, the reality of it crashed over me and my whole body shook. I quickly prayed once again that God would watch over my mom.

It was still dark as we helped Dad into the truck and sped down the gravel road. We pulled up to a house in the village, and Dad began to honk the horn repeatedly. When there was no response, we sighed, hopeless. I realized how terribly alone we were. Would anyone help us?

Knowing we were fleeing for our lives was all too real, and with every mile, I felt a relief and dread all at the same time. Mom's nightmare was still not over.

As the dim light filtered into the cab, for the first time, I was able to see my dad's injuries. I was horrified at the beating he had endured in an effort to protect us from the very abuse we just experienced. There was a gaping hole in his head, and his hand and side where he had been stabbed were bleeding, as well. His face was swollen and blood had dried on his lips. I clutched Jeremy's hand as he sat quietly next to me, wondering again what sort of horror he, too, had endured.

## Darrell

We arrived safely at the American Seabee camp. I told Jeremy to keep honking the horn until I came back for him. I slipped through the cyclone gate and started for the buildings. All of a sudden, two large German shepherd dogs came running toward me, growling. I thought, *I survived a beating, and now these dogs are going to eat me.* Several men came out and calmed the dogs.

"Men broke into our home." I launched into the necessary details of the events as quickly as possible. I knew time was of the essence if we wanted to find Sherri and bring her back to safety. I was sure she was alive, wherever they had taken her.

One man led us toward the infirmary while another went to radio the police. "We'll get a medic to care for you," one of the men assured me. "And we will find your wife." His words were like medicine to my soul.

The friendly faces and the high barbed wire fence brought a sense of security. I was glad my kids were safe and at my side, but the world would not right itself until Sherri was in my arms.

I prayed they would find her quickly and bring her to me. I ushered the kids into the building, where we were promptly greeted by the medic.

While the medic was caring for the kids, I approached a sink and began to check out my head wound. Having worked as an EMT in the past, I took some Betadine and began to clean my wound. The whole front of my skull moved and made a suction noise as a piece of it lifted. Taking a closer look, I realized that I was seeing the lining surrounding my brain. Having worked with similar injuries in the past, I quickly sat down. Poor Jeremy, having to describe my injuries to me! No wonder he and Jadie had looked so sick and worried. It was a miracle I hadn't passed out long ago!

The medic was so kind as he cared for Jadie and Jeremy, gently asking them questions regarding their injuries. Jeremy had escaped with only a few minor cuts and bruises from his attacker. Jadie's injuries, I knew, were primarily due to the abuse she had endured. Again, my heart broke for her, knowing the emotional pain that would follow would far surpass any physical pain she felt.

As I sat there, the events of the night once again began to replay themselves in my mind. I thought of my dear wife, Sherri, and prayed they would find her soon.

I wished more than anything I could jump up and run out to rescue her like a prince on his horse. Sherri deserved only the best, yet I feared she had endured the worst.

*Oh, God, I have to trust You are going to lead the men to her and that she will be okay!*

I felt myself go weak off and on for what felt like hours. Finally, the most wonderful news I could have imagined came over the radio: They had rescued Sherri and would bring her to join us. My heart sang with joy. Sherri had been found! She was alive! Tears spilled down my cheeks as I sank into the chair with relief. The throbbing of my head momentarily disappeared as I praised the Lord for His goodness.

"Thank You, Lord! She's alive! You are so good!" I cried out. The minutes had crawled by like hours as I paced back and forth, not knowing if my wife was dead or alive. A thousand terrible images had flooded my mind during the excruciating wait, but I refused to give up hope that Sherri would return safely. I could now rejoice because our family would be reunited, complete! God was indeed faithful !

I waited for about half an hour when a man entered the room, smiling. "Do you know what kind of woman you are married to, sir? She was singing, singing songs of praise to the Lord all the way here!"

That was my Sherri! Of course she was singing praise songs! Sherri loved the Lord more than life itself. I was not surprised in the least that she was singing through her pain.

My beautiful wife entered the room, clothes rumpled, hair awry. Despite her disheveled state, she was as lovely to me as the first flowers of spring. Tears filled my eyes as I made my way toward Sherri for a long, overdue embrace. I took in everything: her soft skin, her wavering smile, her hazel eyes that shone like a bride on her wedding day. Sherri's tears meshed with mine as we stood there for a moment, comforting each other in our silence. We'd been separated only a few hours, yet it felt like years had passed since we had last held each other.

Jeremy and Jadie rushed to our side, and the four of us held each other through tears of exhaustion and relief. To the world, we must have looked a sight: bruised, beaten and bloody. This mattered little as we clung to each other, silently rejoicing for the miracle that had taken place. As the room disappeared around us, we wept tears of joy and tears of heartbreak for one another. Our stories could wait for another day. Right now, the only thing that mattered was being together. And not letting go.

Outside, I heard sirens and knew the ambulances had arrived to take us to the hospital in Koror.

God had been faithful. He had heard the cries of our hearts during the desperate moments of the night, and He had brought us back together, safe and alive. In that moment, I was so thankful to be reunited with my family that little else mattered.

The dawn of this day ended our treacherous night, but brought with it a whole new world that lay in stark contrast to the one we put to rest the night before. We had a long road ahead of us, and our nightmare was far from over.

# Chapter Three
# THE WORST OF NEWS
# THE BEST OF NEWS

**Sherri**

The ambulance ride from the Seabee camp to the hospital was a blur. With my mind reeling from the night's events, I was weary, weak and overwhelmed.

Yet I was thankful to be with my family again.

We all went to the hospital in Koror, the only hospital in the country. Upon our arrival, a nurse examined Jadie and me. We were stunned by her harsh manner. The nurse spoke about our condition as if she were discussing a dinner menu or television program. I winced as her cold hands met my skin. Looking over at my sweet little daughter, I could see she was just as terrified by this woman as I was.

Darrell was immediately taken for x-rays to determine the extent of his head injuries. In addition, he had suffered stab wounds to his side and his hand that required treatment. After our examinations, Jadie and I were joined by Jeremy in the waiting room where we kept vigil with prayers and baited breath, awaiting the results of Darrell's x-rays.

After what felt like hours, the doctor entered the waiting room and asked to speak with me privately. The look on her face was grim.

"Mrs. Beebe? I'm afraid I have bad news. Your husband's head wound is critical, possibly fatal. His sinuses are crushed, his frontal lobe has collapsed and his brain tissue has been torn, exposing the brain. We cannot treat him here at this facility. He will need to be airlifted to Hawaii for immediate brain surgery. We will keep him here overnight and give him anti-seizure medication so he will be able to fly. However, if he so much as sneezes during the flight, he could get an air embolism and die." She paused. "There is a 40 percent chance he will make it through the surgery. If he does come through it, he will most likely be physically or mentally disabled for life. Perhaps even a vegetable."

My head spun as the words hit me. Forty percent chance? Vegetable for life? My dear husband, always so strong, capable and full of life. I clutched the arm of the chair, feeling suddenly faint.

"He seems to be coherent, though," I protested, "and doesn't show any signs of serious injury!" Darrell and I talked at the Seabee camp, and I was amazed at how alert and functioning he was. How could someone who had done what he did — driving the kids from that house of horrors to safety — how could he require such serious surgery? No. Surely, the doctor was mistaken.

"I'm sorry," the doctor said quietly. "Your husband is in a state of shock, which is why he is still coherent and operating as well as he is. We're going to move him to a general ward tonight, and we'll have him on a flight in the morning. He will need to remain flat on the stretcher in the plane and be accompanied by a nurse the entire way. You'll want to make arrangements for the rest of your family to get to Hawaii on your own. You can expect to spend at least three months there while he recovers."

Three months?! I closed my eyes for a moment, in shock. I simply could not believe her words.

Suddenly a spurt of adrenaline hit me. I had much to do if we were to leave the island on the next flight out.

My mind raced. We were the only Assemblies of God missionaries on the island. I knew another couple, however, Ron and Sharon Thompson, who served as Baptist missionaries in Palau. I knew they would help me with the necessary details.

"Is this the Thompson house? Yes, it's Sherri Beebe. I need your help!" I spoke quickly into the phone, briefly summarizing the horrific events of the past night.

"Oh, Sherri, we're so sorry," was their genuine reply. I

knew from their voices that they were heartbroken for us. "We will come to the hospital at once," the Thompsons assured me.

Jeremy, Jadie and I finished our examinations, and the hospital released us. Ron and Sharon arrived at the hospital, greeting us with warm, gentle hugs and words of comfort. It was wonderful to see familiar faces, especially those of other believers, after the cold treatment we had received at the hospital.

"I need to go to the police department to file a report," I explained. I was operating like a robot, going through the motions without emotion. The tears, the pain and the healing would come much later, but for now, I had to move forward with what needed to be done, as mundane as it might be.

My heart pounded as we stepped inside the police station, knowing that we would have to recount the details of the night. We quickly learned that a large contingent of local men helping the local police had captured our attackers.

"I know you don't have much time, as you have to get a flight out of here. But if you can, please try to recount the events of the night in as much detail as possible," one of the police officers asked us gently.

I looked at Jeremy and Jadie, who stood beside me wearing brave faces. "Just do your best and tell them what happened," I told the children. My heart broke for them, knowing they had endured so much. But I also knew we had no time to waste. We still had much to do before we could head for Hawaii.

"Where did these events take place?"

"Can you remember what the men looked like?"

"Approximately what time did they enter the home?"

The police officers fired question after question at us, which we did our best to answer. Jeremy and Jadie did not falter in their replies, but responded in a matter-of-fact manner to each question. I was so proud of them.

THE WORST OF NEWS ...

"Thank you for your time. We will be in contact with you," an officer informed us as we prepared to leave.

My mind was already moving on to the next thing we had to do. "Thank you," I replied, shaking his hand. I realized mine was trembling, and it hit me just how tired and hungry I was.

Ron Thompson took me back to our house to find our passports and other papers necessary for our trip. My heart was heavy as the car pulled in the driveway. On an ordinary day, I would have taken time to gaze over at the sparkling ocean. Today, however, there was no time for such reflections.

To my surprise, a group of neighbors had gathered at the house to clean up the mess and destruction. Tears filled my eyes as I saw the crowd milling around the property, doing whatever they could to help. I recognized only a couple of them. The rest were perfect strangers to me. They had obviously learned of our tragedy and wanted to do something. *Thank You, God,* my heart cried out.

Outside on the ground, the volunteers laid hundreds of pieces of paper out to dry in the sun. All of our receipts, reports and important papers had been soaked when the men brought the hoses into the house to flood it. Our kind neighbors were trying to salvage our precious documents. I was speechless as I stepped out of the car, taking in the scene.

Suddenly, a breeze picked up. Papers began to scatter in every direction. The people ran toward them, trying to chase each paper down. Again, I was amazed and thankful for their efforts.

"We're so sorry for what happened to you," a woman said kindly, approaching me. "We're here to help in any way we can."

"Thank you," I replied gratefully. I reached out to hug her with what little strength I still had.

We made our way into the house, stepping over broken pieces of furniture and other items destroyed by the attack. I cringed as I stepped into the laundry room. In broad daylight, the scene looked far more horrific than I had imagined. It was hard to believe that just 24 hours ago, we had endured such pain in this house.

Several loads of laundry were scattered on the ground, and I was shocked to see how much blood was on the floor and on the clothes.

I bustled around, packing a suitcase for each of us, trying to think of what clothes we would need for the days ahead. Again I was operating on adrenaline, trying to look past the gruesome destruction and onto what tasks we had to accomplish.

"We have found your passports!" someone shouted outside. Darrell and my passports had been in the hutch in the dining room. The children's passports were being held in the office of immigration while the government awaited their verification and clearance. I praised the Lord that these documents had been found, and that we now were free to leave the country.

With passports and suitcases in hand, we headed back to Koror and returned to the hospital. Darrell had been placed in a large ward with no privacy and very little care. The place was a blur of noise and activity as the family members of patients scurried in and out of the room.

"You look good," I told Darrell honestly. It was still hard for me to believe that a man so alert and conscious was facing a life-threatening surgery.

Darrell squeezed my hand and smiled weakly at me. "You do, too. You're as beautiful as ever," he whispered.

Tears filled my eyes as I let his hand linger in mine. How could this be the end for us? We had been married only 14 years, and Darrell was barely 33 years old. We had a whole future ahead of us, full of dreams that included our entire family. Surely, God would not choose to take Darrell from us now!

I contacted Larry, our friend who was a judge, and

quickly explained our situation. I stressed the urgency for us to be with Darrell on the plane to Hawaii.

"I'll get on this at once," Larry assured me. "I'll contact the president and the government offices to try to get the kids' passports released immediately."

"Thank you so much," I told him, realizing there might never be enough time or thanks to show my gratitude to everyone who had already stepped forward to help our family.

I then went to the airport to begin the job of obtaining tickets to Hawaii for Jeremy, Jadie and myself. From the airport, I called our missionary field director, Wesley Hurst, who lived in Springfield, Missouri. I updated him concerning our immediate need.

"Rest assured, our missions department will cover any expenses you might incur for your flight," he assured me. "Money is no object. Your family's safety is our first priority. We're praying for you," he added kindly.

"Thank you," I replied breathlessly. I turned to the ticket agent at the airport and explained that we would need three additional seats next to Darrell.

"Darrell's unique situation requires him to take up six seats for his stretcher," the ticket agent explained to me dryly. "You'll also need one for the nurse, for a total of 10 seats. That's going to cost you. The first available flight will be Sunday morning."

"That's fine. Money is no object at this point," I replied hastily. "Whatever it takes to keep our family together."

"I'll see what I can do," the agent replied.

If only she knew what we had just been through! Before I could process any more information, we were paged to receive a phone call from the police station. The police requested that we return to the station as quickly as possible to identify one of the men who had attacked us.

"We will come at once," I told them. I could not believe how quickly the day's events were blurring together.

I hardly had a chance to stop and take a deep breath,

much less process what had really happened the night before. We arrived at the police station and met the police investigator.

"I need for you to identify one of the men who threatened and attacked you," the investigator told us.

I realized I was shaking as we sat down in a room across from a lineup of men. There was no glass between them and us; only a few feet of space separated us from our attacker.

I was too frightened and uncertain to identify the man who had hurt us so badly. Jeremy, however, was immediately confident that he knew which man it was.

"That's the one," Jeremy said with resolve, pointing to his tormentor. His voice was completely unwavering, his answer decided.

"Are you sure, Jeremy?" I whispered, nudging him in the ribs.

"Positive, Mom," Jeremy assured me.

I did not let my fears overrule his determination. I was so proud of my son, at 12 years old, mature and strong. I squeezed his hand.

The investigators questioned us for several more minutes and determined that the man Jeremy had picked out was indeed the man who had so brutally attacked us. I was relieved we had taken a step toward justice, but I knew there was much, much more to come. We stood and thanked the police for their time.

Returning to the airport, I knew it was going to be especially costly to pay for 10 tickets but decided we had little choice in the matter. We had to get to Hawaii to be with Darrell!

When we reached the ticket counter, another agent, no more engaging than the first, met us there. "I'm sorry, but the plane is already booked, and I won't be able to put your family on the flight," she told us. "Your husband will go because he is in critical need of medical care. But because the rest of you are not considered medical emergencies, I'm afraid you will have to take another flight. It looks like the soonest we could get you on a flight would be Monday evening. I'm sorry."

My heart sank as her words hit me.

Stay behind and let Darrell go alone?

Doctors would perform his surgery on Sunday. The agent was telling me we couldn't even leave Palau until Monday night?

I could not imagine putting my dear husband on a plane, knowing he faced life-threatening surgery thousands of miles away while I remained here in this terrifying place with two small children.

I fought back tears of disappointment and tried to reason with the woman. "Are you sure nothing can be done?" I pleaded. "Our family has been through much trauma, and we need to be together as my husband faces this surgery. Are you sure no one can be bumped to make room for us?"

The ticket agent shook her head. "I'm afraid not."

Unable to comprehend this bad news, I went to call Darrell's parents, Ed and Peggy, back in Washington. I wanted someone to be there for Darrell in Hawaii, even if it could not be us.

My voice was on the verge of desperation when Mom and Dad Beebe picked up the phone.

After a brief explanation of the attack and Darrell's physical injuries, I asked them, "Please, can you come to Hawaii to take care of Darrell after his surgery? I want to be there so badly, but they can't get us on a flight until Monday evening."

"We'll be there as soon as we can," Darrell's parents assured me. Though they were not avid travelers, I knew they cared about their son more than life itself. His parents would do anything to be by Darrell's side when I could not.

"We'll call Darla, as well," they added. Darla Janke was Darrell's older sister, a strong Christian who I knew could provide a presence of peace for Darrell and his family.

Grateful for their eagerness to help, I returned with Jeremy and Jadie to the Thompsons' home. At this point, the events of the day began to catch up with me. I felt exhausted, both physically and emotionally. I had nothing left to give. The fumes of adrenaline I had been running on were beginning to dissolve, and I felt I would collapse if I accomplished one more thing.

I climbed in the shower and stood under the warm water for some time, letting it wash over my skin. For the first time, I got a good look at the places where the bugs had eaten at my flesh the night before.

I scrubbed at my skin for some time, trying to rub away the filth. Tears burned at my eyes as I recounted the day's events in my mind. There was still so much to do, and so little time!

That night, I climbed into bed, grateful for cool, clean sheets beneath me. I was beyond exhausted and hardly had the strength to pull the covers to my chin. The kids slept on the floor near me, their steady breathing a comfort in the quiet, dark room. I shuddered as the previous night's events flooded my mind.

Then I thought of my dear husband, who would leave us in the morning to face a serious surgery he might not survive.

*Oh, Lord, be with Darrell tonight, and please heal his body!*

I heard a noise outside and pulled the covers closer to me. I was terribly frightened and knew sleep would not come easily tonight. It was hard to sleep in a place where, not far away, such a terrible travesty had reached our doorstep.

Somehow, however, I did manage to sleep fitfully. We awoke early and went to meet Darrell at the airport. We arrived at 5:30 a.m., just as Darrell arrived by ambulance.

He looked worse than he had the day before. Several large bruises had appeared on his face, and his head was wrapped with gauze to make it look more presentable during the long plane ride. Darrell's other wounds had not been washed, and dried blood stuck to various parts of his body.

"I look like half a mummy, huh?" Darrell joked as I met him with an awkward hug.

"You look, well, like you've had better days," I replied, trying to smile. Inside, my heart was breaking for him, and for us.

"I don't need the stretcher after all," he told us. "I have this IV, and the doctors decided it would be okay for me to sit up in the plane with the nurse by my side. So at least that's good news."

"That is good news," I replied softly, trying to be positive.

The owner of our house, our landlord, also happened to be the governor of our island state. He, too, arrived at the airport, along with his wife.

"We're so sorry for the tragedy your family has endured," he told me solemnly. "We want you to know that if there is anything we can do to help your family, we're here to do it. Words can't express how truly sorry we are for all you have gone through."

"Thank you," I replied for the umpteenth time in the past two days. I was afraid my weary state would mask the depth of my gratitude.

The senior Baptist missionary on the island and his wife also arrived and greeted us with hugs, prayers and kind words. Again, I was so thankful that people we hardly knew had come to support us. We stood together around Darrell, a quiet solemn group, as the sun began to rise.

"I promise you I don't feel as bad as I look," Darrell assured us, knowing everyone must be horrified at his bandages and bruises. He tried to be strong, and I tried my best to go along with him. There was no use in falling apart now when he needed us most.

Jeremy had found our video camera and spent the next few moments filming us all as we hugged and said our goodbyes. Jadie, meanwhile, visited with each person in our small circle, showing each one love and compassion. I looked over at her smiling, and momentarily felt a surge of happiness. My children were so brave during their darkest hour, a wonderful example to me of love and hope.

The moments we had together were not enough. Before I knew it, the passengers began boarding the plane, and Darrell was whisked off. A little piece of my heart broke off and died as I gave a weak wave to my precious husband. I didn't dare let myself wonder if I would ever see him again. The courage I had been trying to hold onto for the past day and a half began to slowly melt away as the plane lifted into the air. I pulled my children close to my side and let the tears fall.

Climbing into the van to head back into town, every remaining bit of my strength dissolved. I felt I had truly come to my end. We had barely settled into this strange new land, had endured unfathomable terror and now I was being left alone with two traumatized children and little hope of seeing my husband again.

*God, I have just had enough. I can't take anymore,* I cried out in my heart.

Jeremy, who sat quietly beside me as the van rumbled down the road, suddenly poked me, his eyes excited. "Mom! God just told me that Dad has been healed. He doesn't need surgery!" I could see his excitement as the words spilled out of him.

I stared at my son in disbelief. He had not heard what the doctor back at the hospital had told us. A 40 percent chance of survival! How could Darrell possibly be healed? At that moment, I did not give my 12-year-old son enough credit.

"That's nice, honey," I replied nonchalantly, smiling.

We spoke no more during our ride back to town, but instead lifted our voices up to the Lord, singing songs of praise to Him. For a fleeting moment, I felt the Lord smiling down on us, reminding us of how much He yet cared for us.

There was still much to take care of that day. We went to meet with our church family of Filipino believers to explain to them why we would be leaving the country.

"We don't want you to be discouraged," I told the people as they looked up at us with saddened faces. "We thank you for the love and support you have shown us these past few months and want you to know we will miss you terribly. God will continue to watch over you. He has great plans for you."

Disappointment clouded their faces at the prospect of us not returning. "What will happen to us, and to our church, now that you are leaving?" they asked.

One of the Baptist missionaries stood and announced that he would take over the church and care for the congregants as his own until someone could be sent to help them. It was a relief for all of us.

"We're so very sorry," the congregants repeated over and over, referring to our tragedy. "We will miss you so."

I was touched by these people who had come to love us as we loved them during the short time we had been able to minister to them. I prayed that God would indeed meet their needs in our absence. I had to believe that our time in Palau was not in vain, that God indeed had good plans for us, and for them.

As we trudged through the town of Koror, I was overwhelmed with the outpouring of sympathy and support we received from the Palauans. Word had obviously spread fast, and it touched me to know that the local people, many of whom we had never met before, cared for us. I threw out smiles and waves and more thank yous as we passed by, knowing I was seeing most of them for the last time.

Larry and Elena, our dear friends on the island, took the children and me to lunch at a beautiful resort hotel. It was a wonderful, kind attempt to try to help us feel a bit of normalcy in our suddenly shattered world.

"I think you've got a future documentary maker there," Larry joked, referring to Jeremy and his video camera. Larry tried to laugh and joke with the children in an attempt to comfort their broken hearts.

I stabbed at my food, knowing it was the best I'd eaten in weeks. I was grateful for nourishment but had little appetite. I kept thinking about Darrell and where he must be in his flight.

I tried to smile and make conversation with Larry and Elena, knowing they were trying their best to take our minds off our heartbreak for the moment.

When we returned to the Thompsons' that night, they let me know they had gone back to our house to retrieve the rest of our belongings. I was so grateful not to have to return again to the site of our tragedy. I was not sure I could repeat wading through that horrible destruction again.

"Thank you for all you've done for us," I told the Thompsons once more as I headed to bed that evening. "You two have been lifesavers."

"It was the least we could do," they replied kindly. "And if there is anything else we can do, please let us know."

I slept fitfully again that night, a million thoughts flooding my head as I tossed and turned. My mind was a jumble of flashbacks, prayers and thoughts of Darrell. *Lord, please let him be all right*, I prayed as I finally drifted off to sleep.

Waking Monday morning with a sense of resolve and renewed strength, I slipped out of bed ready to face our last day in country.

There were bank accounts we needed to close and outstanding bills we needed to pay at the hardware store. Suddenly, clearing all of our accounts was very important to me, despite the horror of our situation.

At each stop, sympathetic business owners greeted me. "We're so very sorry for what's happened to you," they told me. "I don't know how you could have suffered so much and still have the courage to go on."

"The God I serve has given me the strength to survive, and He will see me through," I told them. "He gives me grace and mercy so that I can press on." I was thankful that, even in my darkest hour, God could use my small faith to bring glory to Him.

We obtained the kids' passports from the government office that had been holding them, then returned to the Thompsons' home to finish packing our belongings.

Mid-afternoon, the telephone rang. My heart nearly flew out of my chest as I raced for it, sure it was Darrell's parents or the doctors calling with an update. To my utter surprise and delight, it was Darrell on the other end of the line!

"Hi, babe," he said cheerily, sounding as if he was smiling on the other end. "I am okay, and I don't need surgery. God has healed me! It was a long trip through Manila and then to Guam and on to Hawaii. I was 22 hours en route. A team of surgeons was waiting for me at the hospital. Before beginning the surgery, the head surgeon let me know he had seen the x-rays but needed to do a CT scan to give a more detailed picture of the damage. He performed the CT scan, but after careful examination, he quickly realized that the x-rays and the CT scan did not show the same results! All of the previous damage has been healed, and the only thing left on the new scan is a dent in my head. I am going to leave the dent, leave the hospital and meet you tomorrow at the airport!"

I had to sit down to absorb the miraculous news. My husband was healed! I couldn't believe it! Hours before, I had thought I might never see him again, and now he was calling me with the best news I'd ever heard in my life!

"Praise God!" I shouted. "Kids! Come in here, quickly!" I called to the other room. Jeremy and Jadie bounced into the room, and I relayed the wonderful news to them.

"See, Mom, I told you Dad wouldn't have to have surgery!" Jeremy declared, grinning from ear to ear. Not normally pretentious or cocky, Jeremy was especially pleased to be able to verify what God had told him earlier in the van.

*Thank You, God, for speaking through my son*, I prayed through my joyous tears.

I knew, without a doubt, that during our darkest hour, a miracle had taken place. Suddenly, everything changed for me. I knew our wounded emotions would take a long time to heal, but at that wonderful moment, I felt that we could face anything that came our way.

Jeremy, Jadie and I spent our remaining few hours in Palau in a flurry of hugs and goodbyes. We knew that, most likely, we would never see many of these people again, people we had grown to care for deeply in the short time we had been on the island. We shared in their sorrow as we prepared to leave, but rejoiced that we were going to be reunited with Darrell.

That evening, we finally boarded the Air Pacific flight and headed to Guam. The flight to Guam was short and uneventful.

Once we arrived, missionaries John and Marilyn Burke greeted us and took us to their home. We knew we had only 18 hours to spend on the island, but planned to make the most of our time with them.

John, a big teddy bear of a man, took the time to play and laugh with Jeremy and Jadie, trying to provide them with a few moments of childlike fun. They felt at ease with John at once, which made me happy. Meanwhile, I spent time talking to Marilyn, who had a background in counseling.

She gently led me to talk about things I hadn't yet dared to express in words. It was the beginning of the healing process for me as I spilled out everything I had been bottling inside. The tears came, followed by her gentle hugs and encouraging words. I was so grateful for her presence.

Next, we boarded the flight from Guam to Hawaii. I was growing more anxious by the moment to see my dear husband. The minute the plane touched down, I gazed out the window and thought about the many visitors who came to this island in search of refuge, rest and relaxation. On any other day, I might have noticed the sweet fragrance of the flower leis or the succulent smell of the ripe pineapple as I exited the plane. But today, only the overwhelming odor of diesel fumes greeted me as I stepped off.

# THE WORST OF NEWS ...

I was thrilled to see Dad and Mom Beebe waiting for us when we walked into the airport. Darla, Darrell's older sister, was with them, as well. Ginnie Dailey, our friend who had accompanied the children back to Palau, and her husband, John, were standing with them, too. But I looked past them all in search of the one face I was most eager to see: that of my dear husband's.

My heart nearly leapt out of my chest when I saw him standing there, a huge grin spread across his face. His bruising had not yet disappeared, and his lip was still swollen. His head sported a large spider-shaped wound barely held together with two stitches. To me, however, his was the most beautiful face in the world.

Jeremy and Jadie were so excited they nearly danced as they ran toward their dad to embrace him in a long, overdue hug. I followed them, a bit more reserved, and slipped into Darrell's arms. I felt I could stand there and never let go. Truly, God had performed a miracle when He healed my husband. It was nearly too good to be true!

The pastor from Honolulu First Assembly of God had arranged for an apartment where Darrell and his family stayed until we arrived. Jerry Gaffney, whose wife had found my picture in a missionary magazine, arranged for us to stay in a beautiful three-bedroom suite right on the beach for only $25 a night. We were beyond grateful, as we knew the suite normally cost hundreds of dollars a night.

Wayne Cagle, our mission's area representative, arrived to help us arrange for the next steps in our healing process. We agreed that we would return home to Washington State for a   couple days and then go on to Akron, Ohio, where we would be under the care of Dr. Richard Dobbins and Emerge Ministries.

Dr. Dobbins was an ordained minister and psychologist who would be able to assist us as we began to heal, and we would be able to stay nearby in housing provided for us while we went through this process. We felt it was the best move for our family, though we knew we still had a long road ahead of us.

The first night in Hawaii proved to be a miserable one for me. All the poison from the annoying little bugs that had attacked me in the cave finally overloaded my system. I became terribly ill and nearly went crazy with the itching that ensued. A prescription of Benadryl took the edge off, but I was still miserable. Also, trying to sleep put me on edge, as it did the kids. Nighttime was an extremely difficult time for us after our ordeal.

Jadie and I visited several doctors in the next few days, trying to obtain the necessary medical care that had not been addressed while in Palau. We likened our injuries to a car accident where the life-threatening injuries are cared for immediately, but the long-term effects are often overlooked and take weeks, months and even years to heal. We knew this would be the case for us, both physically and emotionally.

One day, I felt especially frustrated and overwhelmed with our circumstances. I ran outside between two tall buildings and screamed, "Why, God?" Heaven did not answer me at that moment, but somehow, I felt better letting it all out.

Darla, Darrell's sister, spent many hours reading to me aloud from the Bible. I found my time together with her especially comforting and loved hearing her read from Romans 8, my favorite chapter during that time.

### Darrell

Swaying along inside the ambulance as it sped to Koror, I was so thankful that our family was together. Badly abused and wounded, but together.

But when we arrived at the hospital, we were immediately separated as I was taken to get x-rays. I did not see a lot of Sherri and the kids in the hours that followed, and I had time to think.

Wesley Hurst was the field director for our area. I desperately needed to reach him but figured it might take a miracle to do so. I first called our headquarters and spoke with a janitor who told me that Reverend Hurst might be reached at Central Bible College.

After phoning the college, I learned that Reverend Hurst was in a special missionary commissioning service and could not be disturbed.

"He is sitting on the platform getting ready to pray the commissioning prayer for the new missionary families," the man on the other line explained.

I urgently relayed that I was a missionary calling from Palau and that this was a matter of life or death. "Please interrupt him at once, even if he is in the middle of a sermon," I pleaded. "This is extremely important."

In a matter of moments, Wesley was on the telephone. I shared with him our situation, and he prayed with us and told us that we had their support and that he would make our need known. I later learned that he returned to the commissioning service and shared what had happened to us and the possible high cost of mission service. The families recommitted themselves to the high calling of God, and he prayed the commissioning prayer.

Since I was facing surgery in Hawaii, the doctor in Palau only used a few stitches to keep my wound together. I was amazed that they never even washed the blood from my head, face or body. I did what I could to clean up. Prior to leaving for the airport, I asked for some gauze. I wanted to cover my wound so it would not be a distraction to other travelers.

I wrapped the entire top of my head, covering the wound and all the dried blood that was in my hair. Early Sunday morning, I was taken to the airport by ambulance to meet the plane. Sherri and the kids met me there.

It broke my heart to say goodbye to Sherri and the kids, not knowing if I would ever see them again this side of heaven. I boarded the plane with the nurse by my side. The Sunday flight out of Palau went through Manila. This was the only way out of the country on Sunday. I was able to stay aboard as the flight crew prepared the plane to fly on to Guam. When we arrived in Guam, I was taken by ambulance to the hospital to be monitored during the six-hour layover before I could fly on to Hawaii.

John Burke, a missionary acquaintance who lived on Guam, met me at the hospital. As we talked, he asked me if there was anything he could do for me. I told him I did not know how long I would be in Hawaii before Sherri would arrive and that I did not have any money. I asked if he could loan me some money. He reached in his wallet and pulled out the only bill he had. It was a $100 bill. He said he wished he could do more but it was all he had. I gratefully accepted the money.

He prayed with me and assured me he would help Sherri and the kids when they came through Guam. We said our goodbyes, and I once again boarded the ambulance and was taken back to the airport for my flight to Honolulu, Hawaii.

The nurse with me on the plane was not much help, as she became airsick. Behind me sat a Wycliffe Bible translator and his wife, who happened to be an RN. We soon engaged in conversation, and I realized once again how God had placed such wonderful believers in my path during even my darkest hour.

The flight attendant was distributing the meals, and I was growing more hungry and thirsty by the minute, but was only allowed to eat ice chips because I was scheduled to go into surgery as soon as I arrived in Hawaii. Nearby, someone began to put pepper on his food. I remembered what the doctor had warned me about the possibility of an air embolism if I were to do so much as sneeze on the plane. The pepper was too much for me, and I knew I was about to sneeze. I braced myself for the coming sneeze and prayed, *Oh, Lord, no! Don't let this be the end of me!* Thankfully, nothing happened, and I remained perfectly conscious and alert for the remainder of the flight.

# THE WORST OF NEWS ...

As the hours crept by, I thought about my dear wife, Sherri, and our precious children. I knew a million thoughts must be running through her mind at this moment, as she was forced to stay behind and take care of trivial tasks. I began to think about the coming surgery and the possibility that I may not survive. I asked a flight attendant for a piece of paper. I needed to write a letter to my family. Tears filled my eyes as the words spilled from my heart and onto the page:

*My darling wife and children,*

*My heart has never been heavier than it was today as I was forced to leave you in Palau. I want you to know how very proud I am of all of you. We never know what we will have to face, but we can be sure that we will never be alone. Even in the times of darkness, Jesus is with us. I would have done anything to keep you from these past few days. I also want you to know that we are a special family that God desires to use somewhere in a special way.*

*I am a little over halfway to Hawaii and am very uncertain of what lies ahead for me. I admit that I am scared, but God will see me through. So far the trip has gone well, and I so long for you to be with me. I have never had to face what I as a father have faced this past week. I only wish it would have been different. I have never faced surgery before, except when I was with you, my love, in Longview.*

*No matter what the outcome, please know that you are and will always be special to me. I know we don't like to think of the worst, but if it happens, all I can say is you have been the best wife and family that God could have blessed a man with.*

*I also plan to be around and share a special love with you that has developed through this crisis. We remember, growth comes through conflict and growing pains are not easy, but we will grow and we will be victorious.*

*Sherri, I know you understand that I did what I could do. I know you do. I long at this moment to hold you close and just let the hours pass. I wish I could express how I feel in my heart toward you. You are loved very, very much.*

*Jeremy, you are my only son. I am so proud of how you stood up under life-threatening times. You are on your way to manhood. I want you to know how much you mean to your mother and me. May you always make us proud of you.*

*Jadie, honey, Daddy loves you dearly. I long so much to comfort you during this crisis time. Knowing what you went through breaks my heart. The only consolation is that this way, you still have a daddy who will do all in his power to live and help you through this time. Remember, Jesus will never leave you. You are God's special child and still His virgin. I love you with all the love in my heart. My life has only been enriched by having you as my wife and children.*

*All my love,*
*Your husband and father (Dad)*
*Darrell*

As the plane descended, I sat up and looked out over the beautiful ocean below. I knew the next few hours on this beautiful island held my fate. I also knew that I served a God of miracles. *God, please, let me see my family again*, I prayed as the plane touched down on the runway.

Immigration officials met me as I exited the plane. I had no passport or documents, so I had to go through a several minute interview before they let me pass through. An ambulance was waiting on the tarmac. They took me to the emergency room at St. Francis Hospital, where a group of surgeons, who had been informed of my situation, were waiting for me. The nurse gave the head surgeon the x-rays, and he looked them over.

"I want to do a CT scan to get a clearer picture of the damage before we operate," the head surgeon told me.

I nodded. "Sounds reasonable enough," I agreed.

I underwent the CT scan, and then lay there, awaiting the results. Again, my mind went to my beautiful family, still back in Palau, which felt like the other side of the world at this moment. How I longed to see them again, to hold them all close to my heart.

*Lord, let this not be the end, but only the beginning for us,* I prayed again.

The surgeon returned a few minutes later, scratching his head in disbelief. "I, uh, it appears that the CT scan results and the x-ray results do not match up." He shook his head, obviously puzzled by the results. "Here I see a crushed skull, crushed sinuses, the whole works, but on this CT scan, nearly everything is completely normal. The only thing I see at this point is a No. 6 dent in your head. This is unbelievable."

"You mean, I'm healed?" I asked incredulously. Could it really be true?!

"It seems so," the surgeon replied, still shaking his head as he scrutinized the CT scan results. He was clearly baffled by the sudden turn of events.

I nearly laughed aloud I was so overjoyed. I was healed!

"Praise the Lord!" I shouted aloud. "Praise the Lord!" What a wonderful testimony to this doctor and to all the world! God had healed my head! Only God could get the credit for something so miraculous!

"I can take you into surgery and remove the dent or you can go back to your room and get something to eat." Surgery or food. I chose food. I returned to my room, suddenly grateful for each moment I was alive.

My friend John Dailey from the States arrived shortly after, and I was able to share the good news with him and his wife. He helped me shave, and I slipped into the shower, and for the first time, washed the blood from my wounds as the water trickled down around me. The warm water was like medicine to my soul. I was healed! My parents and sister arrived and celebrated with us.

Still trying to absorb the unbelievable news, I picked up the phone, my heart racing. I felt like a schoolboy calling his crush for the first time. "Sherri, honey! Listen to this!" I began when I heard her sweet voice answer the phone.

## Sherri

Before we knew it, Saturday morning had arrived, and it was time for us to leave Hawaii. We were headed back to the mainland and good ole Washington State.

As I glanced over the turquoise waters, I again thought of Palau, the island paradise that had promised such excitement and adventure upon our arrival. Our time there had not been what we had anticipated. But I had to believe that in the months ahead, God would reveal to us just why He had brought us there and how He would make good out of this trouble and pain.

# Chapter Four
# THE ROAD TO HEALING

**Darrell**

As the plane descended into Seattle, my mind was a jumble of emotions. Glancing out the window, I saw Mt. Rainier and I realized how wonderful it was to be back home in Washington State. But our visit in Seattle would be short. We were scheduled to leave for Emerge Ministries in Akron, Ohio, in only a few days.

The past seven days seemed surreal. It was hard to believe we had suffered such horror just one week ago. Given the whirlwind of events that took place after the attack, we had not had time to process everything that had happened to us. I was so thankful that God had healed my head injury, but I knew we still had a lot more healing ahead of us in the weeks and months to come.

"It's good to be back in the Northwest," I whispered to Sherri as the plane touched down. At any other time, coming into Seattle would have been a joyous occasion. This visit, however, was bittersweet. We were thrilled at the thought of seeing our family and visiting with friends who had been praying for us, but recounting the events of the past week to these folks would be exhausting and emotional.

Our good friends, Steve and Virginia, met us when we checked into our hotel in Redmond, Washington. Virginia took Sherri shopping for something nice to wear to church the next morning. Knowing there was a good chance our family would be asked to speak, we wanted to look presentable.

We spent the rest of the day with my parents, brothers and sisters, as well as with close friends who felt like family. Every person we met greeted us with a gentle hug and compassionate words.

All tried their best to make us feel loved and at ease.

"We're so very sorry for what you have gone through," one friend after another murmured. "We want you to know we have been praying for you."

The next morning, we attended Sunday service at Redmond Assembly of God Church. Pastor Ray Jennings greeted us and asked if we would briefly share about our tragedy in Palau.

We struggled to keep our composure as Sherri and I walked to the front of the room. "First of all, thank you so much for your love and support. What we have experienced in the past week has not been easy, to say the least."

Briefly, I recounted the attack. I stressed the fact that while a few drunken men had abused and mistreated us, they did not represent the wonderful people of Palau, whom we had come to love.

People in the congregation wept openly as we shared our story. I knew they were hurting with us. Once again, I was reminded of how the body of Christ cares for us in times of need.

After the service was over, I found one of my brothers sitting in his pickup in the parking lot. "Are you all right?" I asked him.

My brother looked up at me with tears in his eyes. "I'm sorry I didn't come in to the service, Darrell," he replied quietly. "But I just don't understand how you can still trust a God who would let something like this happen to you. You were always the good kid. You never did anything bad! You didn't deserve this!" Anger crept into his tone as he finished.

"I know it's difficult to understand. But if I choose to get angry with God, and move away from Him, I will be moving toward the one who came to kill, steal and destroy me rather than toward the one who died for me. Does that make sense?"

He shrugged and looked away. "I guess. I just can't believe God would allow this."

# THE ROAD TO HEALING

Many people echoed my brother's words as we shared our story over the next few months. Some even wanted to go to Palau and become judge and jury. We had a choice: grow angry with God over what had happened, or trust Him, even though we did not understand. We chose to trust.

The next morning, as we prepared to leave for Ohio, our family urged us to stay in Washington. They struggled to let us leave again while they were still dealing with their own reactions to our trauma.

My heart did a momentary tug-of-war. "I know you want us to stay, but we need the help that Emerge Ministries has to offer," I answered.

We knew very little about Ohio and had only recently heard of Emerge Ministries. It was easy to see how our family would think it best for us to stay on familiar turf. But I knew boarding the plane that morning would be the best thing we could do.

"The most effective thing you can do for us right now is to keep praying," I added. "We can use all the prayer we can get."

\*\*\*

The long day of travel from Seattle to Akron, Ohio, proved to be a comedy of errors. Flight attendants began distributing meals, but when they reached our row, they ran out of food.

"We're so sorry about this inconvenience," the attendant told us apologetically. "May we offer you free drinks as compensation?"

"No, thanks, we don't drink alcohol. We'd really like some food," I replied, glancing over at Sherri. Our flight had been delayed, and by now, we were all famished.

"Well, the least we can do is get you a soda," the attendant insisted. She returned with several bags of peanuts and some soft drinks.

We shrugged and accepted the peanuts and pop, reasoning that it was better than nothing. We also accepted the offer of a complimentary meal once we arrived at the airport. Until then, our empty stomachs would have to wait.

After the plane finally touched down in Cleveland, we did enjoy a hearty meal. But then the past week began to catch up to me. Suddenly, I felt very weary and longed for one good night's sleep in a comfortable bed. We quickly found our rental car and loaded our suitcases. Sherri has always been my co-pilot, so she had the instructions we were given.

"All we have to do is find the turnpike," Sherri told me, fumbling with the directions we had written out. The luxuries of Mapquest and GPS were not at our disposal.

"What's a turnpike?" I asked in all seriousness. There were no turnpikes in Washington State, and we certainly hadn't seen anything called a "turnpike" in Palau.

"There's a toll road up here. Maybe that's it," Sherri suggested hopefully.

But it didn't say "turnpike." So we drove around in circles for nearly an hour. After much frustration, we finally pulled over and asked someone about a "turnpike." A turnpike, we soon discovered, *was* a toll road! With that bit of confusion behind us, we finally headed out in the right direction.

\*\*\*

Emerge Ministries had been preparing for us since learning of our attack. Founded by Dr. Richard Dobbins, an ordained minister with the Assemblies of God and a licensed psychologist, Emerge Ministries sought to provide a place of refuge and healing for ministers and missionaries in need.

Though others had faced perilous situations during missionary service, our attack was the worst of its kind where the victims survived. We knew little about what to expect, but were confident we would be in good hands under Dr. Dobbins.

"Our secretary has agreed to loan you her car for the time you are here," one of the staff members told us upon our arrival. "Emerge Ministries has provided a furnished apartment for you, as well. We hope it will meet your needs."

"Thank you so much," I replied gratefully, anxious to rest after our long trip.

The apartment was small but sufficient for our family. A modest one-bedroom, it was sparsely furnished with items donated by the staff, including a dining table and sofa. We were so thankful not to have to worry about basic needs during a time like this.

Two twin camp cots were set up in the living room for the kids. We had all been having trouble sleeping since the night of the attack, so we decided to leave a light on during the night.

"Lord, please watch over our family tonight," I prayed as we held hands together. "We know You are near, and we ask for Your protection as we sleep."

"But, Dad," Jeremy protested, "God *was with us* in Palau, and we were still hurt."

I fumbled for an answer. Jeremy was right. God had been watching over us, but He had also allowed the attacks to take place.

"I know it's difficult, son, but God cares for us. We have to believe He will keep us safe as we sleep." Those last words were for my own reassurance, as well, as I struggled to settle in.

Morning finally did arrive, much to our relief. Beams of sunlight streamed through the window and onto my face. I realized how much we had all come to dread nighttime. Glancing over at Sherri, I smiled groggily. Today was a new day!

"First, let me thank you for giving Emerge Ministries the opportunity to care for your family after the tragedy you have experienced," began Dr. Dobbins gently as we sat in our first meeting with him. "We hope this place can provide the safety, refuge and healing you need during this time. We would like to meet your physical as well as your emotional needs while you are here," Dr. Dobbins continued. "If you have specific medical concerns, we want to attend to those as soon as possible. And by the way, you can call me Doc."

"Thanks, Doc. The Lord has already healed my brain and crushed sinuses, and I know our other physical injuries will heal soon," I told him as I explained the miracle God had performed. Nodding toward Sherri and the kids, I added, "But I know our emotional wounds are deep and will take longer to heal."

We took turns counseling with Doc Dobbins over the next few weeks. He listened intently as we each recounted the horrors we had experienced and the emotions that had followed.

Dr. Dobbins did not prod. Nor did he try to put a band-aid on our pain. Rather, this man of God helped us to open up and try to understand our feelings.

"It's okay to be angry," he reminded me on more than one occasion. "Anger is a natural step in the healing process."

Intellectually, I knew this was true and was thankful for his validation. While I didn't like to think of myself as an angry person by nature, in truth, I *was* angry! In my head and even in my heart, there was no doubt that God was still faithful. But that knowledge did not erase the pain.

Our days were long and restless during the first few weeks at Emerge Ministries. While it was tempting to jump up and "move on," we knew that this was exactly where our family needed to remain for the time being.

Ministry had been our full-time calling since Sherri and I first married. Our kids had never known anything but pastoral ministry and the adventures of the mission field. For the first time, we were able to be together and sit in church as a "normal" family.

Though the emotional wounds were a primary focus for us, the physical wounds were still healing, as well. Sherri struggled during the first few days of our stay as poison from the bugs that had bitten her inside the cave began to seep through her body. This unwanted substance caused her much pain and irritation. Even then, however, we were reminded that the surface wounds were not nearly as painful as the ones inside.

Nighttime remained difficult for us. Whenever we heard a slight noise outside, we jumped.

Darkness itself was a lurking predator.

Each night we prayed for peaceful sleep. I could think of nothing I wanted more than to awake fully rested. It seemed as though it had been years since any of us had had a good night's sleep.

\*\*\*

While our weekdays were spent in counseling and trying to rest, we tried our best to make the most of our weekends by embarking on fun outings. Niagara Falls, Gettysburg, Washington, D.C., and even a local amusement park were just a few of our favorite excursions. Hearing the kids' laughter was like music to my soul. Sherri and I were so thankful for these happy moments that became wonderful memories of an otherwise difficult time.

"Niagara Falls was awesome, Dad," Jeremy said as we headed home one weekend.

"It was pretty amazing," I agreed heartily. The giant cascade of rushing water served as a reminder of just how great God was. A God who created such astounding scenery would certainly not forget about us.

One day, after returning from a theme park, a piece of glass that had been embedded in my foot since the attacks snagged on the carpet. I reached down and pulled it from my foot. I held it up so we could get a good look at it. I was surprised at how large it was. It was the size of a pencil lead and more than a half inch long.

This piece of glass was another reminder of the ongoing healing process.

In the following weeks, each of us experienced our own personal struggles. Jadie, 11 years old, reverted to the age of a 4 year old. We had given her a puppet named Wrinkles, and she began to use the puppet to speak rather than speaking directly to people. On more than one occasion, Jadie slipped under the table at a restaurant and talked back and forth with her puppet.

"Jadie, come on out of there," I tried to coax my daughter.

"In a minute," Jadie replied in a babyish voice, speaking through Wrinkles.

I sighed and glanced over at Sherri. "Remember what the counselor said," I reminded Sherri. "Jadie is reverting to a place where she feels safe because she has gone through such a traumatic, adult event. It only makes sense that she would do something like this."

"The counselor said it could be months or even years before she outgrows this behavior," Sherri murmured, looking weary. "Do you really think that's possible?"

I shook my head. Thankfully, within a few weeks, Jadie stopped using Wrinkles as her spokesperson and returned to speaking directly to us. Sherri and I breathed a sigh of relief, thankful for another small victory.

The end of August rapidly approached. Sherri and I decided it would be best for our kids to attend public school. They were both excited and apprehensive about this new adventure.

"How was your first day of school?" Sherri asked when they climbed into the car. "Did you make any friends? Did you like your classes?"

"It was okay." Jeremy and Jadie practically stumbled over

each other's words as they attempted to relay the day's events. I smiled, relieved that they had so quickly adjusted to life in the "real" world.

It then occurred to me that, to the outside world, we looked like a normal American family going about normal everyday American activities. No one on the outside would ever guess that we had suffered so much pain only a few weeks ago.

Akron First Assembly of God Church became our home church during our stay at Emerge Ministries. We were especially grateful for the wonderful support of the people we met there. Jeremy and Jadie plugged into youth activities at the church. Though we did not know how long we would stay in Ohio, diving into church activities with both feet seemed to be a good way to establish a sense of normal routine in our life.

The pastor met with us one day and asked if we might be willing to share about our experiences with the congregation. "There are so many here who could benefit from hearing what God has done in your lives," he encouraged us.

"We will be glad to share," I replied without hesitation. I knew God would give us an opportunity to share our story many more times in the years to come.

Confident that God had much more in store for our family, I also believed that this was not the end of our story.

One afternoon in the late fall, we received a phone call from the attorney general of Palau. He asked if we would be willing to come to Palau to testify in the trial against the three men who had attacked us.

My heart raced as I thought about what this would entail. We would need to return to the island where we had suffered so much, and come face to face with the men who had terrorized us and changed our lives forever.

"This will be a precedent-setting case," the attorney general explained. "The men have pleaded not guilty by reason of insanity because they had been drinking alcohol, and we want to bring justice to your family. This case could completely change the face of our judicial system."

Sherri and I talked and prayed about this decision. We did not want to put our family through more traumas, but we did not want these men to be free to hurt another family. "The easy thing to do would be to stay here," I said to Sherri. "But I don't believe that is what God wants us to do. We have to believe that He will protect us and that justice will be served." I called the attorney general and told him we would come.

Each day that passed put us one day closer to our departure for Palau, and a thousand thoughts raced through my mind. How long would the trial drag on? How would Jeremy and Jadie respond to everything? What would we feel as we faced our attackers in the courtroom? Would justice really be served?

We had come so far at Emerge Ministries. It had proven to be a safe haven for us. Returning to the island where we had experienced such pain was terrifying in many ways.

While we loved the people of Palau, it was scary to think about being back on the soil where our attackers walked. We knew the culture well enough to know that each person looked out for his own. If one of the attackers had a cousin, brother-in-law or even a friend who learned of the trial, that person could easily come after us to prevent us from testifying. The very thought of going through more trauma was unbearable.

As we told our close friends and relatives about the upcoming trial, they remained supportive. "We will pray that God will be with you and give you strength."

Thankful for their prayer support, we knew we had to trust that the Lord would protect us, both spiritually and physically, as we went to trial. It was not the easy thing to do, but it was the right thing to do. We wanted to go not only so that justice would be served, but also so the people of Palau would see God's love demonstrated through our lives.

# THE ROAD TO HEALING

Much of our free time was spent searching God's word for answers and reassurance. "I found the most wonderful verse," Sherri whispered to me excitedly one evening as we prepared for bed. "Psalm 119, verse 92 says, 'If your law had not been my delight, I would have perished in my affliction.' The law of the Lord is our delight, Darrell! We have to cling to this promise!"

Agreeing, I pulled Sherri close and closed my eyes. My wife's strong faith was a blessing to me during our darkest moments. I had to believe that God would indeed uphold our family during the trial.

Visions of Palau floated through my head that night as I tossed and turned. What would await us when we stepped off the plane? How would God use us during our return to the place we had once called Paradise?

## Jadie

I took a deep breath as we pulled up to our new apartment. It was pleasant looking enough, a two-story building with small balconies perfectly in line. We followed the Emerge staff member upstairs and down a long hallway leading to our unit. Our new house was inside an enclosed hall, much to my relief.

*Perhaps we might actually be safe here.*

Two twin cots stood in the tiny living room for Jeremy and me. A sudden chill ran down my spine as I glanced at the sliding glass door leading out to the balcony. The bars on our house in Palau had not kept us safe, but at least they had served as an attempt to protect us. This large glass door felt like an open invitation for predators. I shuddered and turned away, moving across the room to inspect the narrow adjacent kitchen.

That night, Jeremy and I lay carefully on the cots and yanked the covers tightly up to our chins. I hated nighttime. Every shadow, every noise was a monster, a threat, a reason to stay on guard.

"You okay?" I whispered, glancing over at Jeremy, whose cot was near the sliding door.

"I'm okay," he replied quietly. I knew he was equally afraid. Neither of us had gotten a full night's sleep since the attacks.

Even from across the room, I could see he was trying to be brave for me. We faced each other in an "I'll watch your back, you watch mine" fashion.

I tried to close my eyes. I thought about happier times that did not include bottles breaking in the middle of the night. I tried praying. Nothing seemed to erase the fear. Blinking my eyes open, I called to my parents in the other room. "Mom? Dad?" *Please, please don't be asleep.* Being the last one to fall asleep was worse than sleeplessness itself. Dad hurried into the living room.

"Jadie? Jeremy? You alright?"

My father moved a kitchen chair into the living room and placed it squarely between Jeremy and me. This became the night watchmen's seat, the "prayer chair." For some time, Mom and Dad rotated shifts and stood guard over us until fitful sleep would fall. Many nights they never slept in a bed; they kept one hand on each of us in heated battle in spiritual realms, defending our right to sleep peacefully.

He leaned over, gently stroking my hair. "I'll stay with you until you fall asleep," he assured me. As I tried to get comfortable, my father began to pray for me. He asked the Lord to watch over us as we slept and to give us all rest throughout the night.

After what felt like forever, I finally drifted off to sleep. When dawn broke, it was bittersweet. The joy of surviving one more night and the feeling of being more exhausted than when you lay down eight hours ago. God had not let anything happen to us while we slept! My body ached, however, as though I had hardly slept a wink. When would I finally feel rested again?

# THE ROAD TO HEALING

\*\*\*

My afternoons were spent with the counselor whose office was just across the street from our apartment. The first time I entered the building at Emerge Ministries, I was awed by the grand lobby, complete with ornate floors and beautiful plants.

"You must be Jadie. So glad to see you. Right this way." A friendly receptionist met me in the lobby and escorted me down a long, richly carpeted hall.

A feeling of importance surged over me. Everyone knew my name. And I hadn't even had to sit in the waiting room!

Curiosity overtook me as I wondered what sort of surprises the counselor might have in store for me.

"Hello, Jadie, how are you?" Another kindly woman, whom I guessed to be the counselor, greeted me as I stepped into an office. We sat down at a small table filled with art supplies. "These are for you," she said.

*Am I back in preschool?* I wondered, dipping my finger gingerly into the Play-Doh. As the soft dough meshed between my fingers, I wondered why the counselor wasn't asking about Palau. Surely, she knew our story. Why wasn't she firing questions at me, demanding to know how I was feeling? Perhaps it would come later. I continued to fiddle with the Play-Doh, chatting absentmindedly about anything but Palau.

"Do you like Akron?" she asked as she picked up the red Play-Doh and began to roll it into a ball.

I shrugged. "I guess. It's okay." A quick glance up at the clock let me know I had 42 more minutes to go.

Suddenly, it occurred to me: If I could just make small talk and keep my eyes on the Play-Doh, we wouldn't have to talk about the yucky stuff.

And so I rambled on, telling the counselor about Washington, our family, our apartment, anything except the hurt bottled up inside. Before I knew it, our hour was up. I did it!

The session was finished, and I hadn't shed a single tear!

"Have a piece of candy," the counselor offered warmly, pushing a dish of candy toward me.

"Thanks," I mumbled. Pocketing the candy, I slipped out of the room. Relief swept over me as I walked down the hall toward the lobby.

This system might just work out fine for me. I could come each afternoon, ramble on about school and other trivial things and leave with my candy. Not a bad way to spend an hour.

I tried this tactic for the next week. To my surprise, it worked remarkably well. I kept scrunching the Play-Doh in my hand, and the counselor didn't push me to say or answer anything. And then, one day, she dropped a bomb out of left field.

"Jadie, are you scared at night?" She leaned in toward me, her eyes wide and intent.

The red and blue Play-Doh suddenly seemed colorless in my hands. I let some of it fall to the floor and closed my eyes. *I'm not going to cry! I'm not going to cry! I want to get my candy and get out of here! This isn't fun anymore!*

"Jadie, do you sleep at night? What do you dream about?" Suddenly, the questions were coming at me like bullets being fired from across the room. I blinked back tears I knew were far overdue. I would not cry! Not now, not yet!

"Jadie, it's all right," the counselor prodded gently. "That's what we're here for. To talk."

I didn't want to talk! Biting my bottom lip, I stared at the thick wad of Play-Doh in my hands. The clock in the background went tick-tick, tick-tick, as though it had slowed along with my heart. I felt like a dam, holding back a flood of tears and emotions. If that dam could just stay shut, there wouldn't be a deluge.

At last, the hour ended, and I stood to leave. There was no candy today. But that was okay. At least I didn't have to talk. "See you later," I mumbled and headed toward the door.

"See you tomorrow, Jadie," the counselor replied quietly. I knew she was disappointed.

Each afternoon, the tears threatened to burst forth like Niagara Falls, but I always managed to hold them back. A wall went up in my mind, protecting me from going back to that place where it hurt so badly. If only I could keep holding that wall up, everything would be all right!

One afternoon, my parents took me to Toys R Us, where I picked out a beautiful stuffed dog puppet named Wrinkles. From that moment on, Wrinkles accompanied me everywhere I went. His happy eyes gazed up at me in a permanent smile.

I loved Wrinkles. He never cried, and he was never sad. He was my faithful sidekick.

Wrinkles was a very significant part of my recovery. I had regressed to the age of a 4-year-old girl. This was how my mind chose to cope with life when the pain got too close and I couldn't sort it out.

Wrinkles did all the talking for me and allowed me to feel any way I wanted to without expectations. When I didn't know how to act or feel, Wrinkles handled everything, and this gave me the chance to look at my life as though it was someone else's sad story and not mine.

The regression didn't last for very long and soon, I reappeared as an 11 year old.

As August came to an end, the family began to talk about school. It sounded like a good enough idea to me. We had been to many new schools, and I knew that after the first few days, it would be fun. I had always liked school and was looking forward to the chance to meet some kids my age. This time was a little different, though. What if they somehow knew what had happened to me? Would anyone want to be friends with me now?

I didn't figure Wrinkles could go to school, either. But school was one thing I was always good at and would be something normal in our abnormal life.

"Class, this is Jadie. She is new to Akron. Please welcome her," the teacher announced on that first day. Or at least I think that's what she announced. Her voice was a million miles away, muffled and foreign sounding.

Recess came soon enough. I shyly approached two girls standing by the swings. I had less confidence than usual. Friendships had always come easily to me in the past. Because of our exciting life on the mission field, Jeremy and I constantly had chances to embrace new people.

Now, standing here shuffling my feet on the concrete, I suddenly trusted no one.

With the first day of school behind me, things began to get better. School became a good distraction and most days were filled with fun and good memories.

I woke up the morning of picture day with nothing to wear and a head full of hair that had a mind of its own. I dreaded picture day. The thought of smiling in front of a camera was simply too much to bear.

Standing in front of the bathroom mirror, tears streaming down my cheeks, a sad, tired, very pre-adolescent girl stared back at me. "I can't go to school today!" I cried, wiping the tears away with a wad of toilet paper.

"Then you won't," Mom replied, appearing at the bathroom door. "Put on some jeans and your favorite sweatshirt. We're off to go shopping!"

For the first time in weeks, a surge of happiness flooded my soul. My mom might as well have announced we were off to Disneyland! I felt like I had been paroled.

We spent the day shopping in the historical old Quaker Oats Factory, eating lunch and sipping coffee like two adult best friends. Mom and I tried to suppress our laughter as we ended our expedition with an old time photo shoot.

That day, the clouds seemed to part and rays of sunshine spread into my life. My mom had selflessly put her plans on hold to make me feel like the most important person on earth. I would never forget that special day.

# THE ROAD TO HEALING

***

One weekend, we took a trip out of town. I found myself on the floor of a motel room, tossing and turning. On more than one occasion, my sleep had been interrupted by night terrors. I awoke crying, shaking and sobbing, calling out for my parents. Tonight, I feared, might be one of those nights.

Tears streamed down my cheeks and onto my pillow as I lay quietly on the floor. I stared at the wobbly lamp on the nightstand and willed the darkness away. A quick glance up at the nearby sliding glass door only made me feel more insecure.

Fear washed over my body, suffocating me in the blackness. Nearby, I heard my father's soft words as he stood on "guard," praying for Jeremy and me.

Suddenly, out of nowhere, a vision of Jesus flooded my mind. "Daddy, I see Jesus!" I cried out excitedly. It was as if Jesus was standing right in front of me!

"Where, Jadie? Where is He?" my father asked.

I realized that my father could not see what I saw. "He's right here. He's in a beautiful palace. I see a grand room, at least a hundred feet tall. There are white pillars lining a massive staircase. The only color in the room is a royal purple robe. It's the most brilliant robe you've ever seen in your life! And there's a huge throne on the top of the stairs with pillars on each side of it. Jesus is not on the throne, but His robe is lying over the right arm of it. Jesus is kneeling, weeping and interceding for me. His body is draped with a simple white cloth, and His tears are running down the staircase."

Indescribable joy filled my heart as the vision came into complete focus.

Then, Jesus spoke to me, ever so clearly. "I have never left you. I love you, my child. I will not leave this place of intercession for you. You are always on my mind." With those words, the vision disappeared just as quickly as it had appeared.

Now it was tears of joy that streamed down my cheeks. I had seen Jesus! He was real, and He loved me. No longer did I need to live in a place of fear, wondering if He had forgotten me. He was bigger and stronger than any glass door, than any deadbolt, than any bar on the window. Jesus was my protector and would stand guard for me while I slept!

Just as quickly, the vision was gone. But a warmth and a light remained through the night as I slept in the very arms of my King!

It would not be long after this night, however, that we would receive a call that would again rattle me to the core. Would I have to return to Palau? And if so, would my Jesus remain by my side even there?

# Chapter Five
# THE TRIAL

**Darrell**

Flying from Cleveland, Ohio, to San Francisco, then on to Hawaii and Guam, we crossed nine time zones. We were exhausted to say the least.

The last leg of our trip from Guam to Palau was scheduled to take two hours and cross one more time zone. One hour into the flight, however, the plane lost cabin pressure and immediately descended below 12,000 feet. The captain announced that we would be returning to Guam.

The plane made a safe landing, with the passengers remaining onboard while the mechanics attempted to solve the problem. Soon they assured us that all was well, and again the plane lifted off toward Palau and the trial at which we would testify against our three attackers.

But 40 minutes into the flight, a whooshing sound swept through the plane. It descended rapidly and started banking a turn.

"We're so sorry for the inconvenience, but we must return to Guam," the flight attendant announced. "Please stay seated."

Had we not been so nervous about this trip in the first place, we might have tried to find some humor in the situation. However, there was no time for laughter now. We were already behind schedule, and this delay would only set us back further.

The plane screeched onto the runway and came to a jolting halt. I glanced around at the other passengers and noticed they seemed as agitated as we were.

"Thank you again for your patience," the flight attendant chirped. "The pilot has decided it is best if we use another plane for the remainder of our trip."

Both Sherri and I breathed a sigh of relief. That sounded good to us! By now, darkness had blanketed the sky, and we were growing weary. We got off the plane and joined the crowd in the waiting area.

My mind raced to Palau, where the trial awaited us in less than 24 hours. We would face our attackers in broad daylight! Though we had never once doubted our need to go and do our part, the idea of returning was anything but enticing. I was anxious to get the show on the road so we could return home to the States as soon as possible.

Two hours passed. At last, the announcement: "Ladies and gentlemen, we have another plane ready to take you to Palau." Slowly we stood and filed down the jet way into the plane. Taking my seat, the thought came to me that maybe the third time would be the charm.

I took several deep breaths and leaned back in my seat. Beside me, Sherri smiled and closed her eyes, hoping for some much needed sleep.

*Tropical paradise.* As we descended into Palau, that phrase again popped into my mind. Ironically, we had truly believed we were moving to a paradise when we learned we had been assigned to the island as missionaries. Who would have guessed that just weeks after our arrival, we would endure the most terrifying events of our life?

I glanced over at Jadie, who sat quietly next to Jeremy. My heart broke for my kids, who had already endured so much. I was so proud of both of them, so brave, so mature about our decision to return for the trial. I knew the next few days would be especially difficult for all of us. I prayed God would give us the strength to do what we needed to do.

As we landed in Koror, I could feel the old anxiety building again. It was nearly 2 a.m. by the time we got through customs and out to the main lobby. The police escort and security officers that the prosecutor promised would accompany us to our hotel were nowhere to be seen. My heart sank as I looked around the empty airport. No doubt with the long delay, they had come on time and, not knowing if the flight would arrive at all, had left.

"Are we going to the hotel tonight, Dad?" Jeremy asked.

"Yes, son," I replied wearily. A nice soft bed and comfortable sheets were the only things on my mind at this point.

At that moment, a lone figure came through the main door. R.B. Cavaness, our missionary replacement, greeted us warmly. "I heard the plane fly overhead approaching for its landing and knew you would be here soon. We all were here earlier, but the others eventually had to return to the police station for their shift changes. I'll call headquarters and the security officers will meet us at the hotel. I'll take you there in the truck."

"Great! Thanks so much for coming," I replied, smiling for what felt like the first time in days.

Palau Pacific Resort was to be our home for the next few days. A high-end hotel, it catered to upper-class people who came for the world's finest diving off the shores of Palau. To the average traveler, we probably looked like a typical family embarking on a vacation to paradise. But our visit was definitely not a vacation.

We practically stumbled into the lobby of the hotel, oblivious to the giant palms that waved outside and the ornate floor that echoed beneath our feet. We were weary, physically and emotionally. And we still had a grueling trial ahead of us.

"I'm sorry, but our rooms can only accommodate one bed," the concierge informed us at the front desk. "Your family will need to separate in order to fit into the rooms."

"Oh, no. Don't you have any other accommodations?" Sherri moaned. "It's very important for our family to be together!"

"Yes, please, is there anything you can do?" I pleaded. My mind flashed to the day Sherri had told me she and the children would not be able to travel with me to Hawaii.

Being together was now of utmost importance for our family. How could there be no room with two beds in the entire hotel?

"I'm sorry, this is all we have," the concierge replied, looking less than interested.

My heart sank as I turned to Sherri. "I guess you will sleep with Jadie, and I will share the other room with Jeremy," I told her, shaking my head. "It's the best we can do for now."

Sherri nodded wearily. "Yes, it will have to do," she whispered.

The terrors of night know no boundaries. Whether we were in our cozy one-bedroom apartment in Ohio or this luxurious hotel in Palau, sleep did not come easily. I tossed and turned, waking every so often to check on Jeremy. He slept fitfully beside me. "Lord, please keep us safe," I mumbled as I drifted back to sleep.

The next morning, Wayne and Judy Cagle met us for breakfast. They were representatives of Assembly of God missions and had flown to Palau to support us during the trial.

I was ever so grateful for their selflessness. It meant the world to me to have them by our side on the soil where we had experienced such terror and pain.

My heart thudded as we approached the courthouse.

The haphazard plane ride topped with a restless night had left me especially edgy. A flurry of prayers floated through my mind as I stepped out of the car. Sherri and the kids walked beside me. Each step seemed like 10.

"Remember, the Lord has gotten us this far. He will not leave us now," Sherri reminded me, squeezing my hand as we pushed open the heavy wooden doors.

I nodded. She was right. By now, people were praying for us all over the world. There was no doubt in my mind that the Lord would sustain us.

We met with the prosecuting attorney. He was a kind

man who understood what we had been through but who also wanted to present a strong case that would result in a conviction.

I had assumed we would all be in the courtroom together and testify when called upon. I was a little taken back when the prosecutor said, "We need you to testify separately from your children. We don't want their testimonies to be tainted by anything they hear you say."

"Let us testify first," I replied. "Then they won't hear what we say, and we can be near them when they testify." I thought I had it all figured out.

But the prosecutor countered, "We may need to call you back at a later time. So you can't hear their testimony, either. We feel it would be best if your daughter testified last."

He continued. "We believe her account will be powerful enough to convict the attackers without question. We hope you will find this procedure agreeable."

My heart sank when I thought of my kids alone in the courtroom without us. Trying to protect them from further trauma, I asked if they could testify before the judge without the attackers being present. I was told the attackers had a right to face their accusers. I then asked if the witness chair could be turned so Jeremy and Jadie would not have to look directly at the attackers while testifying. This was finally approved.

I gulped and glanced at Jeremy and Jadie, who sat quietly across from us. They had been so stoic in this ordeal, it was easy to forget that they were still just children. My heart broke once again for Jadie, who would have to face the men who had hurt her so badly. *Lord, please get us through this.*

We waited together in a room near the court while all the preliminaries were completed. Finally, I was escorted into the courtroom. The scene was reminiscent of *Perry Mason*, complete with risers for viewers, a large desk for the judge and a wooden gate separating the witness stand from the podium.

I took my seat, surveying the room. Three defense attorneys and three defendants. All three men were being tried at the same time in order to save time and money.

I shifted uncomfortably in my chair. Ohio seemed a million miles away. *Lord, we have come this far. Please give us the strength we need right now.*

Wayne Cagle smiled reassuringly at me from the risers as though to say, "I'm praying for you." His wife, Judy, had not come to the trial. "I don't want those images to be etched in her mind," he had explained to us. We understood completely.

R.B. Cavaness, the man who had served as an interim missionary in Palau, had come to support us, as well. We were especially grateful for his presence.

"I call Darrell Beebe to the witness stand," the prosecutor announced, looking up from his seat.

Taking a deep breath, I made my way to the witness stand with Jello legs. The moment I sat down, I got a good look at our attackers for the first time.

Three men, ranging in age from mid-20s to mid-30s, sat near the front of the room, facing me. They were taller, larger than I had expected them to be. Because it had been so dark the night of the attacks, I had virtually no recollection of their appearance. I had told Sherri on more than one occasion that I would not have been able to identify them in a lineup. Jeremy was the only one who had gotten a clear look at any of them.

My eyes met those of one of the men for a brief second. I did not see an ounce of remorse, only a cold lead stare.

Earlier that morning, we had met a psychologist from the University of Oregon who had flown to Palau to conduct an evaluation of the three men. His words had chilled me to the bone. "These men showed no remorse whatsoever for their actions," he said. "Most criminals show some sense of repentance after the fact, but they did not flinch a bit."

It was hard to believe these men were so hardened.

Would they crack during the trial, or would they remain emotionless?

As the day wore on, so did my nerves. The prosecutor would ask a question and I would answer, and then he would ask, "And then what happened?" I would respond and he would ask again, "And then what happened?"

The questions continued, one after another. The prosecutor kept asking, "And then what happened?" I would continue and then he would say, "And then what happened?"

I glanced up at the clock and realized I was famished. I had not expected the questioning to be so exhausting. My eyes swept the room, where dozens of Palauans watched the trial.

A few, I imagined, had come out of curiosity, but many had come out of genuine concern for us. Our trial had made headlines locally, in Micronesia and in Hawaii. Many were waiting anxiously for the outcome.

"The court will take a short recess," the judge announced, rapping his gavel on the desk.

I wandered onto the veranda outside to get some fresh air. The beauty of my surroundings was lost on me, the dazzling horizon a mere shadow in the distance. Glancing to my left, I was surprised to see one of my attackers standing less than 10 feet from me. A police officer guarded him closely. My heart caught in my throat.

I stared at the man out of the corner of my eye, taking in his nonchalant stance, his aloof stare into space. Then, my eyes wandered to the gun in the police officer's holster. For a brief moment, I entertained the thought of snatching the gun from his holster and taking the man out right then and there. It would be a swift ending to our nightmare.

Of course, the rational part of me knew better. Seeking revenge was not the answer. Moreover, as a child of God, I knew very well God was asking me to forgive these men. I desperately sought to have a heart of love and forgiveness toward them. At this moment, however, just feet away from the man who had so brazenly attacked my family, killing him was a very tempting thought.

At last, day one of the trial ended. Sherri and I collapsed into each other's arms as we made our way to the car. "This seems far worse than the actual attack," I muttered. "We were in such a state of shock before that the severity of things did not fully hit us. Now, coming face to face with these men, all my emotions are barreling at me like a high speed train."

Sherri nodded through her tears. "Mine, too," she whispered.

Thankfully, we had something to look forward to that evening. The governor of the state of Airai (and our former landlord) had invited us to his home for a special dinner with the local chiefs. We were honored by the invitation. And it would provide a pleasant distraction from the day's events.

As the car rumbled up out of town toward the governor's home, I realized we were going to have to pass the house where we had been attacked. "Kids, you may want to cover your eyes; we are about to pass the house," I called out. "You don't need to see it."

My heart raced as we passed the octagon-shaped tin structure, still standing tall overlooking the water, which had once been our home. It was hard not to relive that horrible night all over again as I accelerated past the house. The flooded floors, the broken glass, the splintered furniture, the bloodstained walls … all part of the nightmare. We had arrived at the house with such anticipation, so ready to reach the Palauans with God's love. When we had prayed, "God, whatever it takes to reach these people with the gospel," we had had no idea what He might allow.

"Welcome!" The governor smiled as he opened his door to us. His eyes were warm as he shook our hands.

"Thank you so much for inviting us," I replied as we made our way into the elegant dining room. "This is a lovely home."

"It is an honor to have your family," he assured me. "You

are very brave to return to the island under these circumstances." The faces of nearly a dozen chiefs greeted us as we entered the dining room. A special meal had been prepared in our honor. We took our seats, feeling like royalty for a moment.

We had hardly taken a bite when one of the chiefs leaned forward, his eyes wide. "I must know, Darrell, how it is that you were able to survive such horrid events? A person with such severe injuries does not usually live through such trauma."

Of course, I saw this as the perfect opportunity to share with these men the great miracles God had performed. I shared about the love and faithfulness of God and how He healed my head.

"There is no other explanation for my miraculous healing. The doctors said I might not live through the surgery and that if I did, I would be a vegetable for life. God had other plans for me, however. He chose to heal me. I did not even need to have surgery. The doctors were all baffled, but I knew the Lord had done an amazing work. We often think that miracles were only performed in the Bible, but I am living proof that God still works them today!"

The men sat thoughtfully, then shook their heads, amazed at my story. I was happy to give God all the glory. I realized that this dinner would be one of the many pieces of the wonderful testimony God was preparing for us.

We had asked the Lord to reach the people of Palau in any way He saw fit, and He was doing just that.

The trial dragged on for days. Each detail we recounted was like a tiny stab to the heart. We had begun such an amazing healing process at Emerge Ministries, but coming here had put the tragedy right back in our faces.

However, we never wavered regarding our decision to go to trial. Revenge was not our motive; justice needed to be served, and we simply wanted to help the nation of Palau set a precedent in their judicial system for those who pleaded not guilty by reason of insanity by using the excuse of alcohol consumption.

"I want you to know how proud I am of all of you," I told my family one evening as we exited the courtroom. My body felt like it had been hit by a truck. I longed for a hearty meal and a good night's sleep. The trial was not only emotionally exhausting, but physically exhausting, as well.

"When do we leave, Dad?" Jeremy asked, looking up at me with weary eyes.

"As soon as we possibly can," I replied. We had no intention of staying in Palau a moment longer than we needed to.

The next day, the court decided to take a break. We were ever so grateful for this reprieve. Our dear friends, Larry and Elena, offered to take us out on their fishing boat. "The warm ocean breeze will do wonders for your soul," Larry told us.

I didn't argue with him. A day on the ocean sounded good after the stifling four walls of the courtroom.

We climbed aboard their boat and headed out to sea. It reminded me of the many days I had spent on the water in the Solomon Islands. I closed my eyes and let the mist spray across my face. For a moment, I felt almost human again.

"Oh, this is beautiful," Sherri said, coming to my side. "I'm so glad they offered to do this." The sun danced upon her face, breathing life back into her weary eyes.

We anchored near a small island shaped like a hollow crater. Jumping off the boat and swimming through a narrow channel, the most amazing sea life greeted us beneath the turquoise waters. It was like an underwater aquarium! I had never seen anything like it in my entire life. Brightly colored fish of all shapes and sizes swam over our legs. Pastel colored live coral dotted the rocks. *It's easy to see why Palau is considered one of the world's best diving spots*, I reasoned as I came up for air.

"Thank you for a wonderful time," I told Larry and Elena as we sped back over the waters that afternoon. "You have no idea what good it did us to get out on the ocean."

# THE TRIAL

"We're sorry you've had to come back under these circumstances," Larry replied quietly. "This was the least we could do. You are dear friends."

But nighttime was still not our friend. We tossed and turned that evening, trying to get some sleep. The beauty of our luxurious hotel was lost on us in the midst of our anxiety. This was no ordinary tropical vacation, but rather an unpleasant business trip. While we were thankful for the kind gestures of our friends during our stay, the stress of the trial weighed heavily upon us.

Compounding our anxiety was the feeling of danger that still loomed in the air. The Thompsons, the missionaries who had so graciously helped Sherri during those days after the attack, had left shortly after we did. After several attempted break-ins to their home, they no longer felt safe on the island.

The one thing that kept us going, aside from our personal relationship with Jesus, was the knowledge that people all over the world were praying for us. Friends, family, other missionaries, even strangers who had learned of our tragedy were bowing their heads and hearts to intercede for us.

Sherri and I were strong believers in the power of intercession. Knowing others were praying on our behalf when we were too weak to do so comforted me to the depths of my soul. A few even wrote us to let us know of their prayers.

Early in September, Sherri had received a letter from Luci, a childhood friend. Though she and Sherri seldom had a chance to talk, they maintained a special bond. The letter was dated July 29th, just four days after our attack.

*Dear Sherri,*

*So far, I have written you at least 12 different letters in my mind this morning. No words will ever be able to fully express my heart's feelings. Even though many years and miles have separated our physical bodies, I still feel that* kindred spirit that goes beyond "just friends." That spirit that caused us to think and feel so much the same, the little things like choosing the same Easter dress or big things like falling in love seem to run from it in a constant flow. I love you dearly. That kindred spirit has been touched by our precious Holy Spirit. You have been so much in my prayers. Wednesday evening I fell under such a heavy burden for you. I found myself weeping uncontrollably. Not knowing what or how to pray, the Holy Spirit spoke for me.

I slept little, cried and cried into the early morning hours but didn't understand why. As I turned to God's word, verses of weeping and warning leaped out at me, but with every verse of warning came a verse of promised strength, protection and courage. Psalm 139 especially stands out to me. It speaks of God's caring about the delicate inner parts of our body. His marvelous workmanship and His constant thoughts being with us whether "I ride the morning winds to the farthest oceans, even there Your hand will guide me, Your strength will support me." In Psalm 138:3, He promised, "When I pray, You answer me and encourage me by giving me the strength I need." I claim these verses; I bless you with them.

Still, as I prayed, I was so overwhelmed by heaviness that I wasn't able to function. I found myself in bed in the middle of the day, not sleeping, but weeping and praying through the Spirit. When Sunday morning came, I wanted to stay home. My eyes were so swollen that no amount of Estee Lauder helped. As I stood in the choir, and Bruce shared with us about your ordeal, I collapsed under the heavy burden of a kindred spirit. At last, I understood the Spirit knew and that's why I share all of this with you, not to add to your burden, but to say to you, the Spirit knew.

I thank my God for every remembrance of you.

Love, Luci

Luci did not know why she was praying, but she was praying at the exact time of our attack. What a precious reminder of the power of prayer. God's amazing timing moved me. It seemed that every time we felt we could not go on, that the night was too long, the pain too much, the hurt too unbearable, God sent a gentle reminder of His love to us.

He had not forgotten us! Day and night, He was watching over us, and all over the world, faithful believers were praying for us. We were truly blessed.

After several more grueling days of cross-examination, the court decided to take another recess. Realizing the huge amount of stress we were under, the police officials wanted to take our minds off things for a bit.

So the police department took us out on their patrol boat for an ocean tour. We were grateful for another chance to breathe the fresh ocean air and escape the stifling courtroom walls.

As we cruised out onto the sparkling sea, I tried to put the past few days behind us for a moment and enjoy the experience. I hugged Sherri tightly as the boat surged over the waves. Water sprayed our faces, and we laughed in delight. Suddenly, to my right, I spotted the most beautiful double rainbow I'd ever seen in my life.

"Look, Sherri!" I said, pointing in its direction. "Have you ever seen anything like it?"

"It's beautiful!" Sherri said. "What a wonderful reminder to us of God's promises. I feel like He put that rainbow there just to remind us that He has not forgotten us in the midst of our pain and trials."

"I agree," I whispered, closing my eyes as the wind whipped at my cheeks. *Thank You, Lord,* I prayed. *You always know just when we need a little hug from heaven.*

Jeremy stood up well under the pressure of the courtroom. The first time he heard "And then what happened?" he almost laughed. We had forewarned him, and it helped lighten the moment. It was a great tension reliever.

After a full day of testimony, Jeremy's presence was no longer needed at court. Judy Cagle agreed to fly with him back to Guam where we would meet him later. He was happy to be finished with the trial. We did not want him to have to stay on the island any longer than necessary. We were grateful for Wayne and Judy, who had gone out of their way to make our unpleasant trip a bit easier.

The next day, Jadie was to testify. The court stood firm in its decision to "save the best for last." The prosecution strongly felt that Jadie's testimony would be the "clincher" in this gruesome case. I knew Jadie was not looking forward to her time in court.

She remained quiet but strong as we headed to court that morning, her head bowed as though deep in thought.

"Honey, just do your best. The lawyers only want you to answer the questions so that they can understand," I said gently, patting her arm. "Just tell the truth. I know you will do well. We will be praying for you the whole time."

Jadie nodded, tears forming in her eyes. *Oh, God, she's just a child!* My heart cried out. I hated the fact that our children had had to endure things far beyond their years. They should be riding bikes with their friends, not testifying against three attackers in a foreign courtroom!

As we left the car and walked toward the courthouse, several reporters shouted questions. We quickly walked past them and into the room where we waited for Jadie to be called into court. The anticipation and anxiety of what was to come could easily be seen in her eyes.

"You'll be okay," I whispered to Jadie, stroking her hair. "You are so brave."

She nodded, brushed the tears from her eyes and stood tall. It seemed to me that she had grown an inch or two overnight. The girlish look in her eyes was replaced with a sad, knowing depth.

"Jadie, we're ready for you," the prosecutor announced.

Once again, my heart broke for my innocent daughter,

who had to endure one of the most painstaking things one could ever be asked to do.

I blew her a kiss and turned to Sherri. "I wish more than anything I could sit next to her in there and hold her hand," I murmured, tears filling my eyes.

But Sherri and I held hands and prayed for what felt like an eternity. When Jadie was finished testifying, she was escorted back to where we were. She ran to us, and we hugged for a long time.

"I hated it, Dad," she whispered. "I hated every minute of it. I kept feeling their eyes on me, and I hated it. I didn't think I was going to be able to go on, but I prayed and felt a little braver and I answered all the questions the best I could."

"I am so proud of you, and the good news is it's all over."

We had finally fulfilled our promise to the people of Palau. Before leaving the court, I thanked the prosecutor, his staff and all the police and officials for their kindness.

"You have gone out of your way for our family, and we appreciate it more than you will ever know," I told them. "This has not been easy, but you have been so accommodating. Thanks again for arranging the ride on the police boat."

The next morning, we prepared to board the plane for Guam and on to the States. We would stop in Hawaii for a couple days before heading to Seattle for a short Christmas holiday with our family.

As the plane ascended into the clouds, I felt as light as the air beneath us. "We did it!" I turned to Sherri and grinned.

"We sure did," she agreed. The color had seeped back into her cheeks, and she looked more relaxed than she had in days. "Oh, how good it will be to be back in the States."

The trial had taken an entire week. When we left, however, the outcome was still unknown. We were fairly certain all three men would be convicted, but the verdict would not be delivered for weeks. Each defendant had been tried on multiple counts, including kidnapping, rape, assault and breaking and entering. If convicted, each man could easily spend 20 years of his life behind bars.

My mind wandered back to that courtroom veranda, where I had stood only a few feet from my attacker. How tempting that gun in the police officer's holster had looked! I was still struggling with my anger and the way the wrong choices of these men had affected our lives. My physical wounds had healed, but I was still dealing with deep emotional wounds.

The emotional part of the healing process would take months, maybe even years to complete. I had chosen to forgive, but I was still struggling with forgetting. I kept reliving the events, and the anger that accompanied these memories continued to boil.

After three precious days of vacation in Hawaii, we were much more rested. As we descended into Seattle, I spotted bright Christmas lights dotting the streets below. With everything going on in our lives, I had nearly forgotten Christmas time was upon us.

Christmas should be a season for rejoicing, a season of love, laughter and memories. This certainly hadn't been the typical holiday season for us. Who would have thought we would have spent the week before Christmas in a Palauan courtroom rather than at home wrapping gifts and decorating cookies?

My parents welcomed us into their home with open arms. The familiar sights, sounds and smells warmed me to the depths of my soul. For now, I was determined to enjoy our time with family and make the most of our short visit.

The night before we were to return to Ohio, Sherri told me of a conversation she'd had with my cousin's husband, Ray. As a child psychologist for the military, Ray was especially adept in dealing with traumatic events.

"Ray said the most profound thing to me," Sherri began excitedly as we prepared for bed. "As I lamented about how difficult it was to forgive and forget, he said to me, 'Sherri,

# THE TRIAL

God did not make us with a 'forgetter." I can't tell you how much this meant to me. Since I was a child, I've been taught that you have not truly forgiven someone unless you have forgotten the incident, as well. He helped me to see that God did not make us with an ability to just forget our tragedies. We can surely forgive, but only God can forget. He *chooses* to remember our sins no more. I feel like a huge weight has been lifted from my chest!"

"Wow," I replied, shaking my head. "That really is profound." I mulled over these words as I drifted off to sleep. *Thank You, Lord, for showing Sherri and me how to begin to forgive. This is not easy for any of us. You are so faithful, though. We want to give You all the glory for our progress so far.*

The next morning, I felt a surge of hope as the Seattle horizon became a mere dot in the sky from my plane window.

We were returning to Emerge Ministries, where we would share some final counseling sessions and allow the kids to finish the school semester.

Jadie and Jeremy sat quietly across from Sherri and me as the plane ascended into the clouds. "Thankfully, we haven't had any more plane problems," I said to Sherri with a wink.

"We haven't landed yet," she replied, laughing. "Anything could happen, right?"

I chuckled. "Yes, with the Beebes along, anything could happen indeed."

With the dreaded trial now behind us, we could look forward to moving back to Washington and getting on with our lives.

We were not sure what the future would hold for us. Would God allow us to go back to the mission field, or did He have something else in store?

One thing we knew for sure: We knew our tragedy was not in vain. What Satan had tried to use for evil, God would use for good.

He had already proven this with the miraculous healing of my head. Yes, I was confident our story had only begun. But how it would unfold? I had no idea.

# Chapter Six
# FEAR AND FORGIVENESS

**Darrell**

With the trial behind us, we were looking forward to the future. We had each experienced a great deal of physical and emotional healing during our stay in Akron, and our departure was now imminent.

Sherri and I discussed the timing of moving back to Washington State and decided that we should wait until the end of the school semester so Jeremy and Jadie could finish their classes.

The Missions department had granted us a six-month medical leave following the trial in Palau. The question now was what was the next step?

I lay back on my pillow, settling in for another long evening. While our night terrors were less frequent than when we first arrived, they still shocked us out of our sleep every now and then. Dr. Dobbins told us we would not often know what would trigger a flashback or night terror. Realizing this was out of our control was rather discouraging, but we learned to face each night with the reminder that God was in control.

Home for me was the small logging community of Forks, a quaint rural town in northwest Washington. "Home," I muttered, my mind drifting to the place where I grew up, where friends and family were just a few steps away. All of this was not part of the "plan." The "plan" was to minister in Palau for as long as God chose to use us there. We never would have dreamed that God's plan entailed a tragedy beyond our wildest comprehension. How would our family adjust while easing back into a "normal" life?

My parents had offered my grandmother's house for us to live in if we would move back to Forks. We could stay there until the next opportunity presented itself. At least it would be free housing.

This appealed to me. It seemed like the most logical thing to do. While the town didn't have much to offer, the incentive of free temporary housing made our decision easy.

I slipped into the living room to check on the children. Jeremy and Jadie slept peacefully on the twin hide-a-beds. Breathing a sigh of relief, I gazed upon their faces for a moment.

Who would have thought sleep could be such a luxury? *Lord, let tonight be a good night.*

February approached, and the children neared the end of their school semester. Sherri and I set about preparing to leave Akron and Emerge Ministries. We made arrangements to stay in my grandmother's house. From there, we would pray about where to go next. I felt like a pawn in a board game, being moved from one square to the next. Upon signing up to be missionaries, we had no idea God was preparing us for such adventure!

We spent our remaining days packing, saying goodbye to new friends and thanking Dr. Dobbins and the other counselors at Emerge. We were truly grateful that we were doing so well, and we were ready to get on with our lives. While we were in Akron, we had purchased a car and were looking forward to the drive across the country.

It felt soothing to be back on familiar soil. We made our home in my grandmother's cozy house and tried to make the most of our time of transition. Our family and friends were excited about our return. Many, we found, were still struggling a great deal with our tragedy. They did not understand how we could find peace and even humor in our circumstances. Humor, fortunately, was something the four of us had learned to rely on amidst our pain. While there was nothing light about our experiences, having a few inside jokes between us was rather comforting.

"Sometimes I feel like people expect us to be the same,"

Sherri observed one day. "And remaining the same is just not realistic. We aren't the same people who arrived in Palau last summer. Through our pain, we have found strength. As much as I want to sometimes, going back and erasing the past few months is impossible."

Sherri's words struck a chord in me. As much as we enjoyed being in the company of family and friends, I realized it wouldn't be long before we would be on the move again. We were growing restless. We longed to be back on the mission field.

I knew Satan wanted nothing more than to quench the work God had begun in us. He would not prevail. We still felt a strong calling to the mission field and prayerfully decided we would go wherever God called us next.

We each had our own set of intense struggles. My struggle was an overwhelming sense of failure. I had not been able to protect my family during the attack. As the leader of the home, this was especially disturbing to me. Though I had done my best to keep my family alive, terrible things had still happened to my precious wife and children. What if we were attacked again? Would I be able to protect my family if another incident arose?

A string of emotions gnawed at me as the weeks crept by. Still struggling with the strong desire to protect my family, I obtained a concealed weapons permit and bought a pistol. I kept it safely hidden in our bedroom should anyone try to break in.

Sherri did not object to my decision to keep a gun. Though we were hundreds of miles from Palau, we were still on edge when nighttime rolled around.

One evening, when the family was away, I heard a strange noise outside my bedroom window. I rolled out of bed and quickly reached for the pistol. Without a second thought, I aimed it toward the curtain. Heart thudding, I waited with baited breath. This time I would not be caught off guard!

As the moments crept by like hours, I finally talked my-self into unloading the gun and putting it back under the bed. I slowly moved the curtain and peeked out into the darkness. A big tomcat ran across the deck and around the side of the house. With a half chuckle, I took a deep breath and climbed back into bed. A cat! To think I'd gotten my adrenaline pumping over a house cat! These days, though, there was no room for taking chances.

Four months after arriving in Forks, we purchased a home about three hours away in Toledo, Washington. After praying fervently about where God would lead us next, a po-sition at a military church in Japan became available. There was no doubt in our minds that returning to missions was the right thing to do. Japan, a buzzing country of millions, was like night and day in contrast to the quiet tropical vil-lages of Palau. What would God have in store for us there?

The Lord was working in me, day by day, teaching me His truths. I knew my journey toward forgiveness was con-tinuing. As much as I wanted to put a band-aid on our tragic wound, I knew this just wasn't possible. Our physical wounds had healed, but we continued to struggle with ongo-ing emotional pain.

Learning to forgive our attackers was without a doubt the hardest challenge. Satan continually threw guilt in my face, accusing me of not forgiving because I hadn't forgotten. I remembered what Ray had shared with Sherri; God had not made us with a "forgetter." As humans, it was impossible to erase certain images and events that had been etched in our minds. This didn't mean, however, that we could not forgive.

One evening, with my Bible propped open, my eyes wan-dered to 2 Corinthians 2:10: "If you forgive anyone, I also forgive him. And what I have forgiven, if there was anything to forgive, I have forgiven in the sight of Christ for your sake, in order that Satan might not outwit us. For we are not un-aware of his schemes."

The words penetrated my heart. It was as if the Lord had

planted them there just for me. I did not want to be outwitted by the enemy. I decided to do some more research in the Bible to find some answers.

During the next few months, our family traveled to different churches around the Northwest, raising financial support for our next assignment. The kind responses of the people who met us at each stop were overwhelming.

Most had heard of our tragedy and wanted us to share bits and pieces about our experiences. A few were surprised at how well we were doing. Several seemed almost offended that we were not more bruised and broken. To see four healthy, smiling people was a bit of a surprise to them.

These rare reactions amused us. While our healing journey certainly was not over, we had progressed by leaps and bounds from the place we were several months back. Choosing to wallow in our pain and suffering was simply not an option for us. We chose daily to move forward, serving God and learning to forgive.

"I could not have survived what you did." Repeatedly, our listeners murmured this response.

"It is only by the grace of God that we are where we are today," we replied. "He gives us the strength and the courage to go on. We are not heroes or super faith people, but God is faithful. It is through Him that we are able to put one foot in front of the other each morning."

A few people made remarks that were more opinionated. "If you had just put more faith in God that night, He would have saved you and your family from this tragedy," one man scolded me one night after a church service.

I was taken aback. The truths of the Bible assured me this was not true, but his words stung nevertheless. That night as we headed home, I told Sherri with a chuckle, "I have to learn forgiveness on a daily basis."

"I know. I'm so surprised by some people's reactions to our story. Some want to make it out to be a bigger thing that it is. We just need to be honest, be ourselves, without turning our story into a sideshow. Keep the focus on God and give Him all the glory for the wonderful miracles He's already performed in our lives."

Indeed, Sherri was right. We were ordinary people in extraordinary circumstances. Our story was unique and powerful, and we would tell it to the glory of God.

Shortly before we left for Japan, I prepared to speak one Sunday morning at a small church in Mossyrock, Washington. After praying a great deal about what to share with the congregation, the Lord put it on my heart to speak about why people suffer. Since our return from Palau, I had found that, nationwide, people struggled with this concept. They wanted to know why bad things happened to good people. Why did God allow babies to die, friends to be hurt, loved ones to be taken away without warning? It seemed there was an overwhelming cry, a yearning to understand this baffling concept. How could a good God allow good people to suffer bad circumstances?

Seated on the platform, moments away from delivering my sermon, I experienced something I had never experienced before or since: I heard the audible voice of God. As clearly as if He were standing right next to me, God spoke these very words: "Darrell, do you really want to know why people suffer?"

There was no mistaking what I had heard. God had spoken to me! I looked up, half expecting to see God face to face. Then I heard myself respond, but I did not speak. "Okay, God, go ahead. I'll bite. Why?" Surprised at the calmness in my own voice, I waited for His response.

And then God spoke again. "When my Son came into the world, I was very concerned about His physical comfort and safety. What men did to Him broke my heart, but I was less concerned with His physical comfort and safety than I was the spiritual condition of this lost and dying world. What happened to your family in Palau was of great concern to me and it broke my heart, but I was less concerned with your physical comfort and safety than I was with the spiritual condition of this lost and dying nation."

I sat quietly as the words sunk in. The Lord had clearly spoken to me! He had a message for me, a message I needed to share with not only this tiny congregation, but with the world! Tears welled in my eyes as I praised the Lord for this wonderful revelation. He had not forgotten me, not even in that dark, damp laundry room, when I lay there not knowing whether I would live or die. He had seen it all, and it broke His heart. Still, He had allowed it, because through our tragedy, people would come to Christ! If this meant one more soul would end up in heaven, my tragedy was not in vain.

As I was introduced to speak, my heart thumped wildly as I stepped to the podium. God had given me the answer to why people suffer. His beautiful words of encouragement made me want to sing! Looking over the sea of smiling, eager faces, I felt a sense of peace wash over me. And I knew just what I had to say.

### Sherri

I peered out the window at the dreary Washington sky and wondered if we were in for another day of rain. It seemed the sun had not poked its head out in weeks. Lying back on the bed, I closed my eyes for a moment, reliving the whirlwind of the past few weeks. We had known it was time to leave Emerge Ministries, and coming here to Darrell's grandmother's house seemed the most logical thing to do. We could rest, get back on our feet and prepare for what God had in store for us going forward.

A million emotions flooded my mind as I lay there under the cool sheets. Going through counseling at Emerge Ministries had sent my emotions on a roller coaster ride. Dr. Dobbins had explained that there were two types of people: those who externalized their anger and those who internalized it.

I had learned to internalize my anger my entire life. The first step toward healing is learning to deal with anger in a healthy way. This was a foreign concept to me.

I was amazed at how much the counseling had brought out of me. Emotions swept under the rug for years began to surface. It was now time to face them and begin a lifetime's worth of healing.

Now here I was, facing new beginnings but still reeling from the pain. Each day was an unexpected journey. Would I awake in the middle of the night from a flashback or a night terror? Would sleep be a friend or a foe? Would I gain enough strength to go about my day as normal, or would fatigue overwhelm me? Fear and insecurity ate at me day and night, trying to take me captive. I had to fight these feelings with the truth, reminding myself that God was bigger than all of my emotions. I had come so far, but my healing journey was far from over.

"Come on, Mom! You gonna get up?" Jeremy's smiling face appeared in the doorway. His rumpled hair and boyish grin put an instant smile on my face. Since the attacks, Jeremy had worked very hard to keep our family happy. He was always ready with a joke, a silly comment or a kind word. I appreciated my son's efforts to keep us laughing. A sense of humor, we had learned, was indeed medicine for the soul.

"In a minute," I replied, tossing the sheets off the bed before I became too comfortable again. "What's on the agenda today?"

"You tell me." He trounced out of the room, laughing.

I sighed and lay back for just one more second. The children had adjusted so well to whatever circumstances the world threw their way. They had tried a new school in a new town and had been cooperative and supportive in our move back to Washington. Returning to a normal life was now a top priority for them. Jadie especially desired to get on with life by returning to school as a normal teenage girl.

Both Jeremy and Jadie still felt strongly about our call to the mission field. Though scarred, our children were not disheartened because of our tragedy. They recognized that God had a great work to do in us, and through us, going forward. When we learned we would be heading to Japan to pastor a military church, we all jumped at the opportunity to serve once again in a foreign land.

"We wish you could stay," our family lamented as we prepared to head out on the road to raise money for our next venture. "The children are doing so well here. Perhaps you should take a break from missions for a while."

"God has called us to missions, and that is what we will do," I replied confidently. Since the attack, my newfound assertiveness had surprised me. Growing up, I had never had much of an opinion about anything. My voice was quickly trampled by the voices of those around me.

Now, I was learning to speak when the need arose. My words were out of love, of course. But my family was often taken aback by my newfound boldness. Where had that soft-spoken woman gone?

The response from others was difficult for me to accept at times. Our family had endured more than most families did in a lifetime. We were a team, united by our tragedy. Outsiders did not often understand our humor and our reactions to what life had thrown at us. And we didn't expect them to. I imagined it must be equally as difficult to be the one watching from the outside in, feeling helpless and wondering if we would ever return to our "normal" selves.

The plane rumbled down the runway and soared into the sky toward Japan. My heart thumped, this time not from anxiety, but out of eager anticipation.

We were excited about our new calling, excited to see what God had in store for us in another foreign country.

As the plane descended, I peered out the tiny window and sucked in my breath. Tall narrow buildings dotted the city, clumped together so closely, the ground was hardly visible.

The scene was a far cry from the jungles of the Solomon Islands or Palau.

We would be pastoring a military church called Yokota Christian Center. The church of 200 met off base and was comprised of mostly English speaking members. It catered to the U.S. Air Force Base. Nearly 30 different nationalities were represented in this church family, we soon learned.

"Wow, cool!" Jeremy pushed open the door to the simple duplex apartment we would call home. "I can't believe we're really in Japan!"

"Just a tad different from Forks, huh?" Darrell teased, setting down the few pieces of luggage we'd brought. "No tall trees and no stream running through the backyard. We're a long ways from home, but we'll find time to go skiing at the famous Naeba Ski Resort."

I smiled and settled into the comfortable sofa. Another adventure for the Beebe family. It felt almost surreal to be back on the mission field. How would the families on base respond to us? Would the children adjust quickly to their new environment?

"You'll need to take the train to school every day," Darrell explained to Jeremy and Jadie. "How does that sound?"

"Really?" Jadie squealed. She was always up for an adventure. "The school is that far away?"

"It's quite a long train ride. About an hour and a half." My body tensed for a moment as I imagined putting my two precious children on a train in a foreign country. Then I quickly reminded myself who was in control. My God had watched over us in Palau, in Ohio and also in Washington. Surely, He would continue to keep watch over us in Japan.

While we enjoyed pastoring the church in Japan, it soon became apparent that the children were not adapting well to their new environment.

During the long train ride to school each day, they were exposed to many uncomfortable things. Pornography was rampant in our part of Japan. Men would often litter the train seats with their smut magazines. Alcohol was also prevalent. It was common for people to get off of work and open a bottle or two with their bosses before they traveled home. The stench of alcohol brought back vivid memories for Jadie, who had come face to face with it for the first time during the attack.

The homework load for Jadie and Jeremy was also intense. Japanese culture encourages students to study for hours each day. They began to get overwhelmed with their responsibilities. Both became depressed.

Tears brimmed in my eyes as I watched them board the train one morning, their feet dragging as though they were made of lead. My heart sank. As much as we wanted to be here, this simply was not working for our family.

"We can't stay in Japan," I whispered to Darrell one night after the children had fallen asleep. "They're not happy here, and they aren't adjusting at all. I wish I could wave a wand and make everything be all right, but it's not."

Darrell had always preached that God was our first priority, family came second and ministry third. Now we were going to practice what he had preached.

After much prayer, discussion and counsel, we decided that it would be better for our family to leave Japan and move back to the States. We made arrangements for Jeremy and Jadie to stay with Darrell's cousin, Jerry, and his wife, Linda, in Wenatchee, Washington. We would remain in Japan until a replacement could arrive. Once again, we found our family separated, but this time, the decision was ours.

That night, as I tossed and turned, Darrell's words played over and over in my head.

*Oh, Lord,* I prayed. *We want to serve You. But we also want to be faithful and care for our children. I don't know what You have in store for us, but You've been so faithful our entire lives. We will continue to trust in You. Thank You, Lord.*

I had no idea what next week, next month or next year held. The lessons of forgiveness, self-worth and security we'd learned were invaluable. The enemy had tried vehemently to discourage us at every step, to make us think we'd come to our end.

But I knew without a doubt that God was preparing us for an even greater testimony someday. We had a story to share with the world, a story of God's glory, faithfulness and healing. Japan was not a detour or a mistake. It was simply a continuation of the wonderful story being carved out for our lives.

As sleep called to me that night, I embraced it. Wherever God called us next, we would go. And He would be waiting there.

# Chapter Seven
# GETTING THE MESSAGE

### Darrell

Unrest can sneak up on you like a stealthy animal. That's what happened to us the summer following our return to the States. We had made our home in Coeur d'Alene, Idaho, taking an associate pastor position at a large church. Several unpleasant events occurring in a matter of just days had overwhelmed us to the point of severe discouragement. One muggy July morning, things came to a head. I found myself on my knees, crying out to God.

"What's going on, Lord?" I called out, shaken with emotion.

Sherri entered the room and sat quietly beside me. "Do you know what today is, Darrell?" she asked softly.

I shook my head. "No, what?"

She pointed up to the calendar on the kitchen wall. "Today is July 25, exactly three years since the attacks."

We grew still for a moment as the reality sunk in. Another year had gone by since that terrifying night! I hadn't even seen it coming. Now, it all made perfect sense.

"Obviously, it's no coincidence we've been experiencing turmoil," I told Sherri quietly, glancing up at the calendar again. The date jumped out like an ugly beast. "Remember, Dr. Dobbins told us anniversary dates might be tough. He said that even if our brains did not remember them, our bodies would. It seems that's what's been happening here."

Sherri nodded. "Wow. Interesting. I guess he was right."

We tried to go on with business as usual, but it was impossible to forget what the day represented. July 25 would always be a marker in our minds, along with birthdays, anniversaries and Christmas. Hopefully, in time, we would be able to celebrate this day rather than mourn it.

In July of 1990, we accepted a call to become the senior pastors at Lighthouse Christian Center in Port Angeles, Washington. The idea of living just 50 miles from where I grew up was especially appealing. Sherri and I strongly desired for the kids to be near family during their teenage years.

We found land in a new development at Lake Sutherland, 20 miles west of Port Angeles. Just 150 feet from the lake, the property seemed the perfect place to build a house and settle down. Jeremy and Jadie had been through so much in the past year. A home that represented fun, rest and relaxation would be the perfect accommodation for their teenage years. We were thankful to God for this great opportunity to live and serve on the Olympic Peninsula.

I had purchased a ski boat from some friends in Coeur d'Alene, and the kids thought Lake Sutherland would be the perfect place to live. The thought of living at the lake and having friends over to ski was exciting. I asked Jeremy if he approved.

The look on his face said it all. "Of course!" he exclaimed. "This is great!"

Jadie was pleased, too. "We're going to have so much fun here!" she announced.

The kids enrolled at Port Angeles High School and adapted quickly to their new environment. I was pleased with their progress after seeing them struggle so much in Japan. Once again, I was reminded of the resiliency of my two teenagers. They had learned to take whatever life threw at them and roll with the punches. Though they remained honest in their struggles, they also embraced new adventures that came their way.

I shared with our church board how grateful I was to be in a place where our kids could just be kids. "They don't want any notoriety. They just want to fit in as normal teenagers like the rest of the gang." The church family was aware of our story, and I requested that they not ask questions of us.

In time, we would share as we felt God directed us to do so.

Over the next few months, I was pleased to see Jeremy and Jadie blend in so well with their peers. It was obvious that they enjoyed their anonymity. Being "normal" teenagers was of utmost importance to them. We built a nice home at the lake, and both kids enjoyed inviting their friends over for a swim in the lake or a trip out on the boat. It was wonderful to see them laughing again, enjoying life as all young people should.

The church I'd been asked to pastor had gone through some tumultuous times prior to our arrival. As I helped rebuild it and gained the trust of the congregation, I continued to deal with my own "rebuilding."

I had come far in the healing process following our attacks, but occasionally, a flashback or dark thought popped into my mind. Satan still loved to accuse me of not forgiving my attackers. However, the Biblical truths I used to battle these struggles proved most helpful. Just as the church could not be rebuilt overnight, neither could my heart. But God proved faithful in both situations.

Shortly after our arrival, the deacon board agreed to repair the carpet in the church sanctuary. It had not been glued down properly, and there were wrinkles large enough to trip the congregants. A large group of volunteers removed all the pews and prepared the carpet to be properly glued down. Our family took the church van and drove to Seattle to pick up 22 4-gallon buckets of carpet cement. We had removed the middle seats in the 12-passenger van to make room for the glue. Jeremy and Jadie were sitting in the back seat for the entire trip.

"Can we come up front with you, Dad?" Jeremy asked, sliding out of his seat. He sat on a bucket of glue between the two front seats, and Jadie sat on a bucket next to him. Just minutes later, as we drove through Discovery Bay, a car pulled out in front of us, attempting to turn left from a right turn only lane.

"Hang on, kids!" I called out, slamming on the brakes. Unable to miss the car, I steered the van and hit it just behind the driver's door. There was a loud crash, and both vehicles slid to a stop.

When the dust settled, we were thankful to be alive but couldn't believe our eyes. More than 40 gallons of glue had broken open, spilling all over the van interior. The thick, cake batter-like substance stuck to every inch of our bodies. Had we not been so frazzled, we might have stopped to have a good laugh.

"Everyone okay?" I asked breathlessly, trying to wade through the goop. I quickly checked on Sherri and the kids and the lady in the other car. Thankfully, our injuries were not life threatening.

Sherri's seat had broken off the stand, and her head had hit the windshield. Jadie's foot was caught under Sherri's seat. I quickly freed Jadie's foot and moved her to the ground.

Moments later, paramedics arrived to help us. They were unsure how to care for us because the glue was everywhere. They wrapped a black wool blanket around Jeremy so he could sit on a seat in the ambulance. Later, when he pulled the blanket off, it stuck to the glue, causing him to resemble a sheep.

Medics placed Sherri and Jadie on backboards. Their clothes stuck to the boards and later, medics had to cut them from their clothing. It took days to remove all the glue. Once again, the Beebe humor kept us going during what could have been a very discouraging and traumatic event.

At church the following week, several people stopped us to inquire about our accident. "It seems that Satan tried to take you guys out in Palau, and now he's trying to take you out again," one member remarked.

I shook my head. "I don't believe that. We just happened to be in the wrong place at the wrong time." I was confident of my words.

We had been the victims of unfortunate circumstances, but we would not stay in a place of discouragement. God had better plans for us.

Often times, Jeremy referred back to our tragedy with humor, as well. "We've been 'Palau-ed,'" he told people. We all found this inside joke rather funny, while others stared back with a puzzled look. They did not understand how vital our humor had become. It was just one of the ways our family remained close, united and strong.

As the years passed, anniversary dates of the attack continued to be an issue. After being blindsided on the third anniversary in Coeur d'Alene, I decided that July 25 would be a holiday for the Beebe family. We would take the day and do something special as a family. This worked fairly well for us, but we still struggled with a heaviness, a kind of mourning. When the seventh anniversary arrived, we decided to stop reacting to the day and became proactive.

In the Bible, the seventh year was a year of jubilee, and the number seven is God's number of completion. We decided to hold a celebration of life; we would throw a party.

Sherri loved the idea. "Let's invite all our friends over for a wonderful time. We will remember how faithful God has been to us through all these years."

The jubilee ceremony proved to be a huge hit. The kids embraced the idea with open arms. We enjoyed a night of praising and worshipping the Lord as we recounted our victories over the past seven years. No longer would we mourn this day! We would look forward to all God had for us in the future. He had carried us out of the trenches and healed us. Our mourning was complete.

We spent nine years pastoring in Port Angeles. During this time, both children graduated high school and married wonderful Christian mates. We were thrilled at how well they had turned out. Jeremy and Jadie had risen above tragedy to become healthy, productive and godly adults.

Meanwhile, God was preparing our hearts to move on

once again. Knowing we would be leaving Port Angeles, Sherri and I prayed and asked God if the time was right for us to return to foreign mission service. Sensing God's direction was for us to remain Stateside, we accepted the position of senior pastor in the small community of Mossyrock, Washington, near Mount St. Helens. The ministry in Mossyrock was rewarding as we guided people into a deeper walk of faith in Jesus Christ.

We also had the privilege of leading several short-term mission trips. I led teams to Austria and Israel, and Sherri led trips to Kosovo and Panama. Together, we also led four trips into Belgrade, Serbia. Foreign missions remained our first love. Since we first married, we had both felt strongly about our calling to serve in other countries. Our tragedy in Palau had not discouraged us from venturing overseas again.

One afternoon, I received a phone call from Rick Johnson, who had been in contact with the missionaries living in Palau. "Darrell, I have a big request to ask of you. Would you consider going back to Palau to share your story with the church there?"

My eyes widened as I sunk into my chair. I was silent for a moment as I took in his words. Sherri and I had prayed and talked about returning to Palau over the past few years. We had never forgotten the country where we had experienced not merely tragedy, but generosity and love, as well. "I'll have to pray about it and talk with Sherri," I told Rick. "I'll let you know soon."

Even as I hung up the phone, I knew our answer. God had been opening my heart toward Palau for some time now. Though I still needed to speak with Sherri, I knew without a doubt that we would return to Palau.

Suddenly, the Lord took me back to a special church service more than 20 years ago. We were traveling to raise funds for our ministry in Japan.

After we had spoken at a service, the pastor approached our family. "God has given me a word for each of you," he said softly. He turned to Jeremy first. "Young man, God told me that you will one day be a worship leader." Next, he turned to Jadie. "Young lady, God wants you to know that He has seen every tear that you have cried during the night, and He is with you."

My heart stopped as he turned to Sherri and me. "God wants you to know that you will one day stand before leaders of nations and share your story. There will even be a book written someday. And Sherri, God has healed you."

Tears filled my eyes as his quiet but powerful words sunk in. I had no doubt God had spoken to this man, giving him a message to share with us. My heart leapt as I realized just how specific and meaningful his words were. Sherri had struggled with side effects after having her gall bladder removed several years prior. I now believed with all my heart that God had indeed healed her, even to the point that she would no longer need to take medication.

And finally, I had confirmation that God would use our tragedy in a mighty way. Though our desire had always been to minister to small communities around the world, God had been preparing us for something much larger. Through our tragedy, God was allowing us to not only reach small islands and communities, but also the entire *nation* with our story of hope and healing. What an amazing privilege! I was beyond thrilled to see how this man's prophecy would play out as the years passed.

With this memory fresh in my mind, I realized God was again bringing His plan together. We truly had a message to share with the people of Palau. It was a message of hope, healing and forgiveness. Undoubtedly, God had a message to share with us, too. Though our agenda lay wide open, I was sure God would fill it with lots of surprises and new adventures.

"We'll go," Sherri agreed at once when I told her of the phone call. "This is so exciting, Darrell! I pray God will use us in a mighty way during our visit. Do you think Jeremy and Jadie and their families will want to come, as well?"

"We will ask them. It may take some nudging, but I have a feeling we're going to be buying plane tickets for the whole clan," I replied with a grin.

## Sherri

To say God worked in mysterious ways in our lives would be putting it mildly. It was a chance meeting. Only God could have arranged our paths to cross again. Our flight had been cancelled, and we were diverted to Houston in order to make a connecting flight to Indianapolis. As we sat impatiently waiting for additional passengers to board, we could hardly believe our eyes.

"Sherri, that looks like Grady and Janet coming down the aisle," Darrell whispered.

"I hardly think so," I replied. "The last time we heard from them they were leaving Cameroon, Africa, and moving on to ministry in Eastern Europe."

Darrell is never slow to make himself known, so he spoke to this attractive couple as they passed by us. "Grady, is that you?" he ventured.

"Hey, Darrell and Sherri, how are you?" Grady's warm Southern accent greeted us.

This flight would only take about two hours, so we quickly decided that Janet would join me in our row and Darrell would sit with Grady.

How quickly the time passed as we shared of our children and our lives. Janet shared that their family had been reassigned to Romania, and then they had moved to Budapest, Hungary. She and Grady had been very busy working with people in the Balkan States. Before we knew it, the plane was descending.

"I am so glad God gave us this opportunity to reconnect," I said.

"Let's keep in touch," Janet whispered as we shared a warm hug and prepared to exit the plane.

# GETTING THE MESSAGE

Just a few weeks later, I heard from Janet again.

"I've been thinking a lot about your story the past few weeks, Sherri. Would you consider going to Kosovo?" Janet asked as I answered the phone on that warm summer day. "I've been praying for God to send someone who can help us reach the women who have been badly abused in the recent war. I believe that through sharing seminars on post-traumatic stress and forgiveness that God can touch them in a powerful way and help them heal. This ministry is strong on my heart, but I cannot do it alone."

Darrell and I prayed, and we knew God had opened this opportunity for me to once again use what the enemy meant for evil to bring glory to God. Five ladies from the church in Mossyrock agreed to travel with me.

At the last minute, we had to change our flight plans due to the bombing of the World Trade Center in New York City. All flights had been canceled. As soon as the planes were flying again, we departed Seattle, not knowing what God had in store.

"I have no idea what to expect," I confided as we gained altitude. Seattle would soon be nothing but a dot on the ground. "This is so different from anything I've ever done before."

"We know God has orchestrated it all," the ladies reminded me. "We can be confident He has a purpose for our trip."

Nothing could have prepared me for the oppression we saw in the desolate land of Kosovo. An almost eerie wind whistled through the deserted and destroyed homes, reminiscent of the emptiness so many of these abused women must have felt.

I spoke at a conference on the topic of hope and healing. My voice wavered as I stood before these precious women, the pain in their eyes so obvious.

"I come here to share good news with you. I know you have been badly abused, and I have, too. But God has helped me to heal and be happy again. He has given me hope to wake up each morning and a peace to lie down at night. He has even helped me to forgive those who have hurt me."

Slowly, carefully, I related my story of tragedy and healing to these women. Their eyes remained glued to me the entire time as tears poured down their cheeks. *Please, God, give me the words. These women may not know You. Use me, Lord, and help them to see how precious they are to You.*

After the conference, several women approached me, still wiping their eyes. "I cannot believe what you went through," they whispered, one after another. They seemed almost more concerned for me than for themselves! I was touched and prayed that even a piece of my story might be an encouragement to them.

As we boarded the plane back to the States a few days later, I could not get these hurting women out of my mind. Things had gone well, but I felt as though we'd touched just the tip of the iceberg. Hundreds, perhaps thousands, of women had been abused during the war. Surely, there had to be a way to reach more of them with the good news of Jesus Christ and the hope, healing and peace that only He could bring!

Not long after we returned from Kosovo, Janet called again.

"Your testimony was quite powerful," she told me excitedly. "I wonder if you might consider going to Serbia this time. There are many hurting women there who need to hear the same story you shared in Kosovo. Please pray about it."

I prayed, indeed, but God had already been pressing on my heart to return to the Balkans. This time, Darrell would travel with me, and he would have the opportunity to speak with men. His message would mirror mine: You are victims of a terrible injustice, but God can heal your broken hearts and your homes.

The program's organizers had rented out a 1930s hotel

ballroom in the heart of Belgrade, Serbia, for our seminar. The hotel boasted ornate cathedral ceilings and thick, beautiful doors, evidence that it had once been an elegant place before the veils of communism had covered it. We had no idea how many people would attend, but we were certain God would be faithful whether one or 100 walked in those doors.

"We want to make them feel like royalty," Janet had said while preparing us for the seminar. "Many of these women came from well to do families and are highly educated. They had beautiful homes, lovely clothes and fancy food. We want to recreate a bit of that for them again. We'll arrange to have elegant food waiting for them when they arrive. It's important for them to feel loved and important. I know you and Darrell will do a wonderful job conveying that to them."

Many of these women, we learned, had left their homes with only the clothes on their back. Now they were refugees living with their entire family in a 10 by 12 foot room, unwanted and forgotten. How tragic! *Please, God, use us once again to reach these people with Your love.*

The seminar went more smoothly than I could have imagined! As I spoke with the many beautiful women who poured through the doors, I learned that their stories were all very similar. The cycle of hatred had continued for years and years. Revenge was all they were taught. Forgiveness was a foreign concept to them.

The Lord gave me a connection that I felt might help these women understand what I had been through. With the help of an interpreter, I shared how my little girl and I had been abused by men whose mothers were probably abused during World War II.

"But the good news is, instead of continuing this cycle of hate, we can choose to forgive and move on. God can help heal our wounds, no matter how deep or how permanent they seem."

Jadie stood at that moment and had a chance to share her perspective with the women. She gave an eloquent speech far beyond her years. Tears filled my eyes as she spoke.

"I, too, have been a child who was hurt. Instead of hurting back, I have chosen to forgive. I've found true freedom in doing this. It does not always feel like the easy road, but the peace that overwhelms you is unlike anything you've ever experienced."

One by one, the women wept. Most of them had not heard the good news of Jesus Christ, much less been introduced to the concept of true forgiveness. As I stood facing them, tears spilling down my cheeks, I praised the Lord. Once again, He had used our tragedy for good. What Satan had tried to quench, God had used in a way more powerful than we could have imagined!

The love and compassion of these women was truly overwhelming. Several women were taking turns hugging Jadie. One precious lady said, "We will not be able to remember your name because the sound is so foreign to us; but we will call you 'Hope' because that is what you have brought to us."

Meanwhile, Darrell had the amazing opportunity to speak with the hurting husbands of these women. "Many of you are dealing with the effects of wrong choices of other men. You are trying to help your wife through that, but some of you abused other men's wives during the same war," he told them.

"You have repeated the cycle of hurt and abuse as a result of sin in your lives. The good news is that you no longer have to go on living this way. God can break your chains and free you from this cycle. You can experience true life in Christ and the amazing peace of true forgiveness!"

Slowly, the men bowed their heads, and Darrell knew he had hit a nerve. These men were open, ready to surrender.

Exhausted and overwhelmed, we returned home after just five days. We had shared in four women's seminars and two for the men. Each meeting was wonderful and terrible as we listened to the painful stories of many hurt and wounded hearts.

# GETTING THE MESSAGE

A few weeks after we had returned to the States, the phone rang after midnight. Half awake, Darrell fumbled for it. "Hello?"

It was the colonel who was working with the refugees. "I apologize for calling so late. I could not wait to share the good news with you, though! I want to thank all of you for coming to speak to these people. What you said has made an impact on them. They are not drinking alcohol anymore, they are not doing drugs anymore and they are finally able to sleep through the night. What you have done has helped so much. Please come back."

Now fully awake, he stared at me past the phone, speechless. We thought things had gone well, but had no idea we had made such an impact! *Thank You, Lord! To God be the glory!*

We were asked to return to Belgrade three more times. Each time, we shared the same message of hope with a different group. And each time, we saw lives changed. Hope returned in the eyes of those who once had none. Only God could have arranged something this beautifully!

"Isn't it amazing?" I marveled to Darrell as we again boarded the plane for the States. "Our minds are so small. When we left for Palau, we had no idea God was weaving such an amazing testimony for us to share. I feel so blessed by our incredible journey!"

Little did I know that the biggest adventure yet awaited us just around the corner.

## Jeremy

*Another first day at another new school.*

I sighed and glanced at Jadie. Slinging our backpacks over our shoulders, we stepped out of the car and bravely ascended the steps of our next academic home.

"Good luck today, Jeremy," Jadie called out with a wave as she went in one direction.

I waved back and headed the other way. A lump formed

in my throat, but I quickly dismissed it. New schools were something Jadie and I had grown quite accustomed to during the past few years. Initially, it was a bit tough to be the new kid, but we eventually fell into our routine and found our place. Friends always seemed to come easily to me wherever we went.

As I slid into my chair in my first period class, my mind wandered back over the past couple of years. While Mom and Dad finished out their missionary commitment in Japan, Jadie and I returned to the States to live with our aunt and uncle for a couple months. We attended school in Wenatchee, Washington. Being separated from our parents was more difficult than I had imagined, but somehow, the four of us survived.

After three long months, our family was reunited, and we moved on to Coeur d'Alene, Idaho. I obtained my driver's license at only 15 years of age and was delighted to buy my first car and tool around town.

Our next stop was Port Angeles. Now a junior in high school, "real life" was just around the corner for me. I was fine with that. The silliness of high school didn't appeal to me much. I was ready to get on with life and start a family.

Port Angeles proved to be a wonderful experience for my sister and me. I had dabbled with football in Coeur d'Alene, knowing it was the American thing to do, but found it wasn't really my thing.

I was most comfortable on a pair of water skis, skates or a bike. I made many friends that year and enjoyed a wonderful summer on the lake near our house.

Trust remained a big issue for me. I had always been a planner and felt that God had let me down in Palau. I dealt with this by trying to keep a backup plan in line at all times. If there was a backup plan, I would not feel that I had failed.

Maintaining peace in my family was also extremely important to me. This often came in the way of a silly joke or a kind word of encouragement. Our experience in Palau had catapulted me to a maturity far beyond my youth. My concern for my family often came before my own needs or feelings. In essence, I was never the same after Palau.

In 1993, I married my high school sweetheart, Jennifer Kiesser. Jennifer was a wonderful, godly woman, and I looked forward to pursuing ministry with her and starting a family. Five years into our marriage, God blessed us with our beautiful son, Bradley. Life felt complete.

"I feel like God might be leading us to Boise, Idaho," I told Jennifer one day after church. "I feel a little vulnerable trusting my plans completely to Him, but I really feel the need to give everything over to Him."

"Then let's pray about it, Jeremy," Jennifer encouraged me.

We spent the next few days in prayer. I had recently made several career changes and continued to struggle with trusting God. I wanted to know that if I chose to follow His lead, that it would be the right thing, the best thing.

How could I truly know for sure? What if He let me down? Somehow, that nagging doubt always lingered in the back of my mind. After all, Mom and Dad had felt called to Palau. But it was there that life had changed for us forever.

One evening, as I sat praying and reading my Bible, I felt the Lord strongly encouraging me to trust Him. I took the plunge. *Okay, God, I trust You. I want You to lead us as a family. I will go if this is what You want for us. And I will trust that Plan A is what You have for us, without looking for a Plan B as a backup.*

The moment I relinquished my plans to the Lord, I felt a wave of relief wash over me. It was as if years of bottled up fears had suddenly evaporated! Even if things did not go as "planned" in our next venture, I could trust that it was still indeed the Lord's plan for our lives.

We moved to Boise and became youth pastors. From there, Jennifer and I moved to Texas and worked with Acquire the Fire, a nationwide ministry to youth.

We then returned to Boise. I felt frustrated with ministry and the limited income and decided to take a job in sales. God continued to bless our home.

Our second son, Brandon, was born and we were financially successful. I had accepted another traveling ministry position, and we decided to move closer to our family.

One day, I called Dad and asked him if he thought it would be all right if we moved to Mossyrock to be closer to them. He said, "Give me a second to pray about it — yes!"

We spent four years in Mossyrock and started our own ministry called J3 Ministries. Our focus was sharing with churches and leaders a message of God's true desires for a relationship with Him.

"How would you feel about returning to Palau someday?" my father asked me one day over the phone.

My heart skipped a beat. "I don't think I could go back to a place where I experienced so much pain. It wouldn't be healthy," I replied without much consideration.

"Pray about it," my father encouraged me. "Maybe someday you will change your mind."

As I hung up the phone, I was quite confident that I would not change my mind. Palau was a thing of the past, a place where our tragedy began, a place where our dreams had been shattered. It made no sense to think about returning.

One August, I retreated to the mountains for a week to spend some alone time with God. It was then I felt Him strongly impress upon my heart the need to vocalize my forgiveness for our attackers in Palau. I had forgiven them in my heart years ago. But I now felt He wanted me to say it aloud. I obeyed the Lord.

As the next few hours passed, a strong burden to pray for Palau swept over me. Initially, I was not sure where this strong desire came from, but I could not ignore it. I found myself weeping and praying for all the people of Palau. Through my tears, I cried out for the souls of our attackers.

Slowly, God gave me just a glimpse of His compassion for these people. I saw them through different eyes: the eyes of Jesus. They were in desperate need of a Savior, just as we all are. Their sin was no different than my sin. What they had done was horrid, yes, but God still loved them and did not desire them to perish.

"Palau will be your inheritance," I heard the Lord say to me. His words were so clear that I could not mistake them. *My inheritance! Oh, Lord, what are You preparing me for?!*

With the wind rustling softly in the tall evergreen trees, I closed my eyes and wept like I hadn't in years. At that very moment, my heart began to soften toward the people of Palau. I cried out for their souls, asking God to save them. And I knew that God was preparing me to return to Palau.

As I headed home, excitement mounted in my veins. I could hardly wait to tell Jennifer what God had shown me on that mountaintop! I could not get God's words out of my mind: "Palau will be your inheritance." The very place that had caused me so much pain was to be my inheritance!

What would await me in Palau? Would I really get a chance to share God's love with my attackers? How would they respond? How would God prepare me to share with them? Though a million questions circled my mind, I now knew one thing for sure: When God called me to go, I would go.

## Jadie

My heart caught in my throat. *No. Not again!* I gripped the steering wheel fiercely with both hands and tried to breathe. He was there again. The ominous black figure in the backseat.

*Lord, no! Please, no!*

Slowly, I dared to glance in the rearview mirror. There he sat, a silent, uninvited passenger. Dressed in black from head to toe, his face was a blur beneath a dark black top hat. I shuddered and turned back to face the road. With trembling fingers, I reached over to fiddle with the radio. Perhaps a Christian song would drive him away.

To my dismay, static filled the air instead of comforting praise songs. My heart sank.

Before me, the road became a blur of frightening images. To the left and the right, strange figures darted out of dark trees. It was like a scene straight out of a horror flick. My knuckles turned white as I hugged the steering wheel in a death grip. *Jesus, help me!* I tried to utter the words, but nothing came out of my mouth. Like a robot in slow motion, I kept my eyes on the road and prayed this nightmare would end.

"Jadie, what are you doing out here in the dark?" Suddenly, my father was beside me, his eyes full of concern. "Come in. It's late."

"Where am I?" I asked, snapping out of my daze.

My father shook his head. "Your car. In our driveway. You look as though you've seen a ghost."

"I, I think I have," I replied quietly. I didn't believe in ghosts, but I did believe in spiritual attacks. I firmly believed Satan was trying to sabotage me with fear. Each night as I embarked on the 20-minute drive home from work, Fear himself followed me. I became so overcome with fear that I could scarcely remember how I got home. This pattern continued for six terrible months.

At 16, I had come a long way since our attack in Palau. The move to Port Angeles had proved to be a wonderful change for our family.

Within a few months, Jeremy and I made many friends at church and at school. We spent weekends water skiing on Lake Sutherland near our house. These were memorable, fun times.

I enjoyed the anonymity of our new town. My father, being sensitive to our needs, had requested our story not be told at our new church. Therefore, only a handful of people knew what had happened to us in Palau. This left Jeremy and me to live life as two normal, thriving teenagers amongst our peers.

When I turned 16 and began driving, the stranger in the backseat began to follow me. He terrified me to no end. I lay awake at night, aware of every creak of the floor, every rattle of the window. At times, I heard footsteps outside my room, and then, a dark presence seemed to come through the door.

He came to the foot of my bed, where he stood breathing heavily over me. I tried to scream for my parents, but again, no words came out. My legs and arms were immovable, leaving me helpless and terrified.

One night, my father found me on my bed, curled into a fetal position, rocking back and forth. "Don't hurt Mommy! Don't hurt Daddy!" I cried, sobbing.

"Jadie, what's going on?" My father put a gentle hand on my shoulder, which I quickly slapped away. He was my attacker and had come to harm me!

"Get away from me!" I screamed, clawing at his arm. "Get away from me!"

"Jadie, it's me, Dad," my father whispered softly, pulling away.

I shook my head, my eyes wild with fear. "No! Get away from me!" Shaking and sobbing, I curled back into a ball. It was as if I was back in the house in Palau, surrounded by my attackers. I was thankful I had godly parents who knew how to pray and how to love me through these times.

These incidents — living nightmares — were frighteningly real to me. They continued for months.

My mother took me to a wonderful Christian counselor, who encouraged me to journal every day. "You must learn how to fight back with scripture and truth," the counselor advised me. "You are a child of God, and Satan cannot harm you. You must rebuke these evil spirits with the powerful truth of God's word."

For the first time, I realized I truly was engaged in a spiritual battle. I had grown up hearing about such things as spiritual attacks, but had never personally experienced anything like this. Though years had passed since the actual attacks in Palau, Satan wanted me to live as though they had happened yesterday. He wanted me to remain stuck in a place of fear for the rest of my life, crippled and unable to do God's work. God had good plans for me, though, as He had promised in Jeremiah 29:11. I would not allow Satan to pin me down like this! I would fight back, just as a soldier going to battle would do. I would arm myself with the truth of God's word. And Satan would not win!

Day by day, I fought this very real battle. Each time fear approached me, I fought back with scripture. Eventually, the incidents subsided. It was a great relief. Slowly, life returned to normal, or as normal as it could be in the Beebe household.

I tried out for cheerleading and was delighted when I made the squad. Being a leader at school and being active in the youth group at church proved to be very fulfilling. I continued to work, attend school and spend time with my friends. Life was good.

After graduating from high school, I attended a six-month YWAM (Youth With A Mission) school. There I met my husband, David, and we married a year later. I was thrilled to find such a wonderful, godly man for my life partner.

Not long into our marriage, however, our physical relationship became an issue. I found that being physical with my husband triggered flashbacks of my attack.

"You can trust me, Jadie. I love you," David continually repeated.

"I know, I know," I cried. Slowly, I began to recount to him the awful details of the attack. It was important for me to let him know what had happened that night, so that he might understand why I struggled now.

As the words spilled out, so did the tears. It felt good to be honest with my husband, who I knew loved me dearly. I did trust him, but fear had been deeply embedded in my heart since that terrible night.

Together we prayed daily, and I promised to tell him everything I was feeling and when I was scared, and slowly, everything began to make sense to me.

I began to invest my emotions into my marriage and went forward with confidence. I was not that hurt little girl anymore! I was happily married and excited about my life and my future.

David joined the Army and was a chaplain. When he deployed to Iraq, I moved with my two boys to Washington to be with my parents. Our third son was born while David served overseas. Following David's return, we accepted the call to be senior pastors of Vineyard Church in La Porte, Indiana.

One day, my parents called me with an important request. "We've been asked to return to Palau," my dad told me. "Will you pray about traveling with us?"

I sucked in my breath. Return to Palau? No, thanks! I had come so far in my healing journey. I had a happy little family of my own. Palau was a million miles away, a bad dream of the past. Surely, God wasn't asking me to return!

"I don't think I could, Dad," I replied firmly. "Why? Are you really going?"

"I believe God wants us to go," my father replied. "Pray about it, Jadie. You don't have to give me an answer tonight."

*My answer is no*, I wanted to scream as I hung up the phone. *God, surely You wouldn't ask me to return to a place that held so much pain for me! I've come so far! Setting foot on that island again would be like reliving the horror all over again!*

For days, I tossed and turned, unable to sleep. Nightmares plagued me, and I found myself with no appetite. *I've been obedient to everything You've asked me to do in the past*, I told the Lord. *Surely, You don't want me to go!*

After seven days, I clearly heard the Lord speak to me.

"Jadie, you have been faithful. There is no unfinished business. I only want to bless you there!"

God then gave me a promise from Psalm 84:6: "As they pass through the Valley of Baca, they make it a place of springs, the autumn rains also cover it with pools." The valley of weeping would now be a refreshing spring upon my return.

I breathed a sigh of relief as the tears fell. God wanted me to go to Palau not so I could relive the pain, but so that He could pour out His blessings on me!

Excitement now mounting in my veins, I picked up the phone.

"Dad? I believe God's given me an answer."

# Chapter Eight
# RETURN TO PALAU

**Darrell**

"Look, Darrell!" Sherri could hardly contain her excitement as we entered the Palau Airport terminal. "Look at those beautiful Palauan believers! And that banner!"

A crowd of nearly 50 Palauan people had gathered in the terminal, awaiting our arrival. They raised their hands in songs of praise and worship as we strode toward them. A big banner read "Welcome back Beebes to your Palau. What a mighty God we serve." My heart soared as I realized they had all come just for us. We'd only been on Palauan soil a few moments, and I already knew God had great things in store.

"Welcome! Welcome home!" One by one, the people made their way toward us, embracing us and showering us with plumeria leis.

I felt highly honored with this demonstration of love.

"It's so good to be here," Jadie sighed, accepting one hug after another. Beside her, Jeremy, his wife, Jennifer, and their two boys, Brandon and Bradley, embraced our greeters with open arms. What a wonderful welcome we'd already received!

The next few moments were a whirlwind of hugs, songs and tears. Aubra, the photographer we'd brought with us from the States, took several pictures to capture the emotional moment. It felt a bit surreal to be back in the place that had pressed on our hearts for so many years.

Twenty years had passed since we had been back for the trial. That visit had been filled with painful emotions of anxiety, apprehension and uncertainty. This time, our hearts were filled with joy, excitement and anticipation.

"It looks like our luggage is on another plane and won't arrive for a couple hours," Jeremy informed me. "Should we head to the hotel, anyway?" He nodded toward his two young sons with a wink. "I know these guys are up way past their bedtime."

I stifled the yawn I'd been suppressing all evening. It had certainly been a long day, and we had a busy week ahead of us.

Tomorrow was Sunday, and we would be sharing in the church service. A good night's sleep would do us all good. "Let's head to the hotel and hope our bags arrive soon," I agreed. "We have a big day tomorrow."

A couple hours later, our luggage arrived, and we all settled into bed at the Airai View Hotel. As my head hit the pillow, a smile crept to my lips. The past few months had been a whirlwind of excitement as we prepared to return to Palau. After confirming through prayer that God did indeed want us to return, we contacted our children to ask if they might want to join us. Their initial apprehension turned into excitement as the weeks passed. Jadie had planned to bring her family along, but at the last minute, plans changed, leaving her to fly solo. Jennifer and Jeremy had decided to bring their boys along for an experience of a lifetime. This excited me greatly. We had also invited our dear friends, Steve and Virginia Bjorklund, to travel with us. We knew they would be a strong support for us spiritually and emotionally.

With the passenger list in place, it was now time to raise the funds for our trip. After learning how much it would cost for us all to travel to Palau, I seriously began to wonder how we would raise such a large amount of money in such a short time. Praise God, we raised the money after visiting only four different churches. Truly, God had provided and wanted us to go to Palau!

I had prayed a great deal about what God specifically wanted us to accomplish during our trip. God pressed 2 Thessalonians 1:11-12 on my heart more than once: "We constantly pray for you, that our God may count you worthy of His calling, and that by His power, He may fulfill every good purpose of yours and every act prompted by your faith. We pray this so that the name of our Lord Jesus may be glorified in you, and you in Him, according to the grace of our God and the Lord Jesus Christ."

My honest prayer was that God would be glorified through our visit and that we would be able to reach the lost nation of Palau with the good news of God's love. We did not return as victims of a terrible crime, but as survivors with a message of love, hope, healing and forgiveness.

Shortly before we touched down on the island, Jennifer had tearfully shared a vision God had given her between Guam and Palau. "I saw the country of Palau, and God's voice was singing under it through the earth. His voice was a deep, passionate wail, authoritative, but sweet at the same time. Then I saw the kingdom of God, a large clear diamond-like castle coming up out of the ocean all around Palau. He said, 'My kingdom is manifesting all over the Earth.' I saw Palau being pushed up out of the water inside this kingdom of God and light beams breaking up through it." What an amazing picture of God's plan for Palau!

It had crossed my mind several times that we might encounter our attackers during our stay. Two of them, we learned, had been sentenced to nearly two decades in prison for their crimes. The third had escaped from prison about a year after the attack. After six weeks, the police hunted him down. When they found him, they exchanged shots and he was killed. I was saddened initially by his death, mainly because I feared he had died without hearing the good news of the gospel.

"But he did hear it," Sherri shared with me. "I told him when I was in that bunker during the attack. Whether it penetrated his heart, we will never know, but he did hear of God's love that night." Her words had overwhelmed me.

Even during the most painful night of her life, my wife had shared the gospel with one of her attackers! Perhaps we would get the chance to share with the other two men on this trip, should we meet them. Having a chance to extend our heartfelt forgiveness toward them would be wonderful.

"Lord, I pray You will use us to reach the people of Palau in a mighty way," I whispered with the last shred of energy I could muster before sleep called to me.

Morning came all too soon. I awoke, thankful for a good night's sleep. "Thank You, Lord," I exclaimed as I stepped out of bed. I had briefly wondered if sleep would be an issue for our family this week. Thankfully, God had granted us all a restful night void of any anxiety or fear!

When we pulled up in front of the Palau Assembly of God Church, I couldn't help but grin. Twenty years ago, we had held our meetings in the shade of a humble chicken coop, then in a simple rented building. Now, there was a beautiful building, complete with electricity, running water and sturdy walls. As we filed in one by one, I noticed everyone removing his or her shoes. We slipped ours off, as well, and paraded in.

"We want to thank the Beebes so much for coming this morning," Missionary Dale Eytzen shared as the service began. We were overjoyed to hear the beautiful worship music both in Palauan and in English.

Then, the governor of Airai, asked to speak, stepped to the front of the church and smiled in our direction. "It is such a pleasure to have you here. On behalf of the people of the State of Airai, we want to offer our sincerest apologies for what took place here many years ago."

We all rose and made our way to her side. "Thank you so much," we replied, one by one. We tried our best to accept the apology graciously, knowing it was necessary from a cultural standpoint for this to take place.

In our minds, an apology was not necessary at all. By God's grace, we had long ago forgiven our attackers.

"Thank you all so much. You are very kind and gracious," I began. "We have never felt attacked by the people of the State of Airai, but by three men. We have fallen in love with Palau and have been praying for this country for many years. It is truly a blessing to be able to stand here with you today."

Jennifer, Jeremy's wife, then moved to the keyboard. "God has given me a special song for the people of Palau," she began. "I hope you enjoy it." She cleared her throat and began:

*I saw heaven open*
*There was Father God*
*Holding in His hand*
*A precious pearl*
*He held it like a baby*
*Closely to His heart*
*With such compassion*
*He sang this song*
*He sang for you*

*This is my Palau*
*Oh, how I love them*
*They are precious to me*
*This is my Palau*
*Oh, how I love them*
*They are my pearl at sea*
*I'd pay any price*
*For my Palau*
*I saw God the Father*
*Sending down His power*
*Breaking all the chains*
*That held you down*
*Palau shown like a jewel*
*A sparkle in the sea*
*God the Father dancing*
*While He sings*
*He sings for you*
*Tell them of my love*

# DARKNESS AT DAWN

*Show them of my power*
*The Love of God the Father revealed*
*He sings to you*
*He sings to you*

As I looked out over the congregation, I saw many wiping their eyes, clearly touched by Jennifer's precious song. "We encourage you to come back this evening for another service," I said. "We are expecting God to heal many people."

After the service, several church members asked us to pray for two elderly members of the congregation. They had both suffered for years from debilitating physical conditions. We prayed over them both, and instantly, they were healed.

"Praise the Lord!" I shouted. Never once would I underestimate the power of the Holy Spirit!

Little did I know, this was only a taste of what was to come in the next few days.

That evening, the church was packed again for another amazing service. This time, Jeremy spoke. He spoke from Psalm 103 on the goodness of God. I was proud of the confidence and excitement about the Lord that shined forth from him.

Many leaned forward intently, hanging on every word with tears in their eyes. When Jeremy finished, he invited attendees to come to the front for prayer.

"I believe God has another amazing healing work to do tonight," he declared. "If you need a miracle in your body, now is the time to ask the Lord to do His work." I waited, scanning the room with anticipation.

Many people came forward to be healed. One woman was totally deaf in her left ear. As I reached to pray for her, she was touched by the power of God. "I can hear, I can hear!" she cried, jumping up and down excitedly.

Following a prayer, Sherri noticed a young woman trying to see her reflection in the window. She appeared to be looking at her back. At last, her husband joined her and touched her spine. She then burst into tears. "I have had very bad asthma since a child, and my spine curved as I grew. All my life, I would feel great pain if I stood straight. Now, I am standing straight without any pain!"

Another young woman began to rejoice. She explained that she was an Olympic athlete and had won multiple medals in the Micronesian Games in Saipan in 2006. Her knees had given her terrible pain for some time. Without anyone even touching her, she was healed from her pain. She began to dance around, praising the Lord for His miraculous healing.

The service continued for four hours. By 10 p.m., 31 people had been healed. We could only attribute this miraculous event to God Himself. We knew we were not healing evangelists, but merely ordinary people with a strong faith in God. He had heard our prayers and had delivered these people from their anguish. We could not have been more elated!

Monday morning arrived bringing with it a fresh rain. We awoke, rested and excited for what the day had in store. The church arranged for us to take their bus on a three-hour tour of the island of Babeldaub, home to the nation's new capitol buildings. Pastor Regina, the former first lady of Palau, would serve as our tour guide.

As we rode, Jennifer and Pastor Regina engaged in a fascinating conversation. "I was raised Catholic, then entered a Baptist church and then became Pentecostal," Regina began. "My husband was the first president of Palau. He was assassinated several years ago, and I harbored great resentment toward the men who killed him. I knew one of these men when he was a boy and could not believe he had been the one to pull the trigger on my husband. I wanted him to suffer and die just like my husband had." Her eyes grew sad as she spoke.

"Then, God helped me to see that I needed to forgive my husband's murderers. He took me on a long journey, and I was able to truly surrender to Him. I even had the chance to forgive my husband's murderers in person a couple years ago."

"Wow, that's amazing!" Jennifer replied in awe.

I shook my head in disbelief. God had once again orchestrated a wonderful conversation between two believers. How wonderful that he had taken Regina on the very same journey he had taken us on many years ago!

"What is the best thing we could do to help Palau while we are here?" Jennifer asked.

Regina paused to think. "Evangelism," she said decidedly. "And discipleship. The people need to hear God's word and be discipled in it. That is most important."

We reached the top of a tall hill overlooking the ocean. I sucked in my breath as we stepped out of the bus. A warm tropical breeze met me as I gazed out over the vast ocean. It was so unlike the chilly, rugged beaches off the coast of Washington. No words could describe the awesome beauty of this magical island.

Once again, I thought of how perfectly God had orchestrated our lives. The attack hadn't seemed like part of the plan at the time, but we could now see how He was beginning to bring our lives full circle. To think we were back visiting this place 21 years later nearly blew my mind.

"This place is amazing!" Jeremy exclaimed as we walked around the campus of the capitol building. A lone, graceful structure, it outshone anything we had seen thus far on our trip. "I see such promise and a great future for Palau," he added as we stood side by side, enjoying the view.

That evening, we were asked to go to the prison in Koror to speak to the prisoners there. My heart skipped a beat as I learned of this request.

"Lord, I told You I was up for anything this trip, but I'm just not sure I can do this," I prayed alone in the hotel room. "Please show me what to do."

As I prayed, I felt the Lord impress upon my heart the need to go. I stood at last and took a deep breath. "Okay,

Lord, I will go. I promised You I would use every opportunity for Your glory, and if this is part of the plan, I will go. Surely, You must have a purpose for this visit. I will trust in You."

Jeremy and Jennifer came to my room. "Ready, Dad?"

I nodded. "I wasn't at first, but I am now. I'm sure God wants us to share with the prisoners."

Aubra, our photographer, went along with us. "God, Your will be done in here," I prayed once again as we came to a stop in front of the prison.

Unlike American prisons with televisions and freshly painted walls, this prison resembled something straight out of the 19th century. We entered through a side door and wound our way through a dark, muggy alley. The stench of urine filled my nostrils, and I nearly choked.

Pastor Ruth, the prison pastor, led us to an open courtyard surrounded by an upper level where we could see into the higher security prison cells. The courtyard was the basketball court for the prisoners, as well as their dishwashing area.

A microphone, speaker and keyboard had been set up for us on a 5-gallon bucket. Beside the keyboard, another bucket served as a stool. Contrasted with the beautiful church we had set foot in the night before, it was like night and day.

Slowly, many male prisoners and a few female prisoners filed into the courtyard and took a seat. They sat in silence, waiting for us to speak. A chill went up my spine, as the atmosphere seemed to have turned quite dark. I prayed once again that God would give me the words to share with these souls who desperately needed to hear of God's love.

A few ladies from the local church showed up and sat near Jennifer. She made small talk with them while I sat on the makeshift stage. When at last it seemed all had arrived, Pastor Ruth introduced me. I cleared my throat and began.

"I really don't want to be here," I began. "I don't like prisons. But you probably don't want to be here, either." This opening statement set the prisoners and I at ease, and I began my story.

"More than 20 years ago, my family and I came to this island as missionaries. After being in country only nine weeks, our home was broken into in the middle of the night. We were beaten, kidnapped and abused. My injuries were severe, and I was not expected to survive. The fact that I stand before you today is a true miracle of how great our God is.

"He has not only healed my physical wounds, but my heart, as well. I have learned the importance of forgiveness and have forgiven the men who attacked us and overcome my anger toward them. This is all by the grace of God."

I continued to share about God's love, how He has made a way for us to be forgiven for what we have done. As I spoke, the men began to nod their heads. I noticed a few wiping their eyes.

I prayed silently that God would break through and touch their hearts.

I introduced Jennifer as she stood to sing the songs she had written about Palau. Approaching the keyboard, she nearly knocked over the bucket, providing momentary comic relief.

"I am happy to be here," she began. "I had a vision from God about this prison some time ago. In my dream, I saw a prison with brown-skinned prisoners seated in rows and chairs. I was with a team, and I knew that I was singing music for them. I saw the Holy Spirit come down and heal many of their bodies and emotional wounds. Many asked Jesus into their heart as their Savior. I know God cares for you. He loves you so much that He gave me this vision and sent me halfway around the world to share it with you."

Jennifer sang a song called "The God Who Sees Me," which reflected on the good she had had in her life, as well as the mistakes she had made. "I sing this song for you because God has shown me that, despite my mistakes, He still loves me, even sending His son to die for me. He can do the same for you. He can make you a new creature, despite what you have done in the past."

As she ended her song, the atmosphere in the courtyard began to change. The prisoners erupted into applause. It did my heart good to see them respond so positively to Jennifer's song.

"I have one more for you. This is called 'My Palau.' God gave me another vision of Palau that inspired this song. In this one, I saw God the Father in heaven, holding a pearl like a baby, singing this song to the people of Palau. I hope you enjoy it."

Her voice was like that of an angel as it wafted through the courtyard, landing on the hearts of this stone-faced group. I prayed fervently that God was doing a good work inside each one of those hearts as she sang.

Jeremy then rose to preach. Once again, he impressed me with the ease with which he spoke. He seemed so comfortable sharing with the prisoners, as though they were his peers.

As Jeremy concluded his message, he said, "My God is a personal God who loves you and cares for you. He wants to heal you not only spiritually, but physically, as well. If you have a physical need and are in pain right now, please come up front, and my God will heal you."

It took some time for the first person to move, but when he was instantly healed, others began to follow.

In a few moments, eight men were healed.

Jeremy continued praying, now asking for healing for the men in solitary confinement on the second floor. When Jeremy instructed these men to see if their pains were gone, the men began waving their hands through the bars and rejoicing. Jeremy then gave the men the opportunity to ask Jesus to forgive them for their sins and ask Jesus to become the leader of their life. Twelve men responded and for the first time asked Jesus to forgive their sins. It was a beautiful time of both spiritual and physical healing.

Suddenly, God spoke clearly to me with words I will never forget: "Darrell, had I not withheld my hand 21 years ago, these men would not have their names written in the Lamb's Book of Life. When their eternal soul was on one side of the scales of time and your comfort and safety was on the other side, I withheld my hand and the scale tipped in their favor. But remember, when your eternal soul was on one side of the scale of time and my Son's comfort and safety was on the other, I withheld my hand and the scale tipped in your favor."

I was deeply moved as these words permeated my heart. It was a true "Aha!" moment as I realized just how much God loves us. His heart had broken for us during our suffering, but He had allowed it so that, years and years later, we might return here to share with people who desperately needed the gospel message. God had allowed His Son to suffer so I could receive His forgiveness, and He allowed us to suffer so these men and women might hear and respond to the message of God's love. God's plans are always better than man's!

Jennifer stepped to the microphone once more. "I want to share with you one more thing that I was reminded of by God. In my vision, I saw a big, tough man with lots of tattoos. He was a leader of some kind. He had a heart of stone, but I saw God place in him a new heart and heal the entire trauma of his childhood. I saw this man in orange clothing, but I don't see him in the crowd right now. I pray he might come to know Jesus. I also pray that any dark, evil forces in this place might be dispersed and that God's angels be released here in their stead."

As we prepared to leave the prison, a Palauan woman approached us. "I was so excited when I learned you were coming," she said excitedly. "I remember clearly when you were attacked 20 years ago. At the time you were living here, I was a tarot card reader. When I learned of your attack and how you continued to trust God despite your hardship, it impressed me so much I accepted Jesus as my Savior. I gave up tarot card reading for good. Today, I work with Pastor Ruth here at the prison and continue to attend church and serve God."

I shook my head in amazement. To think we had left such lasting impressions on people we had never met! "Thank you so much for sharing that," I told her. "What a blessing!"

Tuesday morning, Sherri and I decided to return to the house in which we had lived. When we arrived on the property, I noticed a young man walking by who looked to be about Jeremy's age.

"Excuse me, but can I ask you a strange question? How old are you?" I said.

The young man stopped in his tracks. "I am 32, why do you ask?"

I paused. "Twenty years ago, we used to live here. Do you remember the Beebes?"

The young man's eyes grew wide. "Why, yes, I remember, I used to play with Jeremy and you made us cookies! My name is Magellan."

Magellan's big brown eyes grew sad. "I am so sorry ..." His voice trailed off. "I heard Jeremy was ... killed?"

I shook my head, smiling. "No! No! Jeremy is quite alive. In fact, he's just a few miles away at the Airai View Hotel."

Tears filled his eyes as he shook his head. "I thought for sure Jeremy had been killed by those men! I would love to see him!"

"And I'm sure he would love to see you," I assured him. "Can you come with us back to the hotel?"

"I'd love to," he responded with excitement. What a wonderful reunion Jeremy and Jadie had with Magellan.

Later that afternoon, we drove to the trail leading to the largest waterfall on the island. Locals had told us it would be only a 20-minute hike, but it proved to be twice that.

However, the beautiful cascading waters that met us at the bottom of the hill made the hike well worthwhile. The waterfall spilled into a river flowing on smooth old lava rock. Several natural pools shimmered around the waterfall. The beauty of the area was breathtaking. I had never seen anything quite like it.

"This is so cool!" Jeremy's sons, Bradley and Brandon, cried. "Can we swim in it, Dad?"

"You bet!" Jeremy replied.

We all took turns swimming in the crystal clear water at the base of the waterfall. After emerging from the pools, we climbed onto a nearby rock to pray. Around us, a slight breeze rustled through the dense trees, and somewhere off in the distance, a bird called.

"Lord, we could not ask for more right now," I prayed. "We praise You for allowing us to set foot back on this land. May Your will be done this week." My heart felt full as I opened my eyes and gazed back toward the waterfall. It was only day three, and already God had done so much! Just as the waters poured down over the hillside, so had His blessings poured down on us.

*Thank You, Lord!*

Finishing the last leg of the hike, we took a break under a thatched shelter. We spoke with the man who was selling tickets to the waterfall. When he learned who we were, his eyes grew wide. "I was 17 when that happened. I clearly remember getting the news of your attack that day," he told us somberly. "I'm so glad you are alive and well today." We invited him to attend our outdoor crusade, and he said he would try to come.

As we climbed back into our bus, I turned to Sherri and mused, "You know, I didn't realize our attack had made such an impression on people. I suppose it was one of the most devastating events to take place on this island. Kind of reminds me of when we learned President Kennedy had been shot. Everyone seems to know just where they were the minute they heard the news."

As my head hit the pillow that night, I could hardly sleep. This time it was not due to fear, however, but to anticipation of what was yet to come. God had done amazing things in just a few short days, and we hadn't even started the crusades yet! I could hardly wait to see what more He would do when crowds of people came to hear the message of hope, healing and forgiveness we offered.

I was reminded of verse 20 from the book of Ephesians, chapter 3: "Now to Him who is able to do immeasurably more than all we ask or imagine, according to His power that is at work within us." Indeed, God had done *immeasurably* more for us than we could have ever hoped or dreamed.

The next evening, we held a dinner reception for government officials in the hotel where we were staying. We wanted to honor them for their kindness and generosity toward us.

Senators, legislators, governors, chiefs, as well as the president and vice president, had been invited to the dinner. It was perhaps one of the most intimidating events we had ever hosted, yet one of the most exciting. Our goal was not only to thank them, but also to share the same message of hope, healing and forgiveness we had shared with many others since our arrival.

One by one, we shared our testimonies with these amazing people. Jeremy shared his vision from the mountaintop months prior, when he had felt the Lord tell him Palau would be his inheritance. Jadie shared how her innocence had been stolen the night of the attacks, but she also felt that, in a way, Palau's innocence had been stolen that night, as well.

"I love this country and have grieved for it just as I have grieved for myself," she explained. "But God is good. It is a dream come true to stand before you all tonight."

The meeting grew quite emotional. I shared briefly how God had worked in my heart, helping me to forgive my attackers. Sherri shared her message of hope and forgiveness, as well. The leaders sat quietly, dabbing at their eyes. It was quite humbling to see such powerful people moved to tears over our stories.

Jennifer sang the song "My Palau" for everyone. They absolutely loved it.

She then presented a painting she had painted titled "Peace from the Northwest" to the vice president. He was especially touched, as artwork has a special significance for the Palauans.

After our good friend, Steve Bjorklund, sang "It Is Well with My Soul," the vice president stood. "I want to apologize on behalf of the entire country," he began. "I must commend you for the love and forgiveness you have shared with us. You have truly touched us."

"You are each in a wonderful position to influence this country for Christ," I replied. "You have the potential to influence this nation in the will and way of God. We will be praying for you all and for a great revival in this land."

"I must tell you that many of our government officials were invited by the president to attend a Federal Aviation Administration Conference," one senator told us.

"I came here because I do not need more information about politics or science, but because I need to learn more about forgiveness. So thank you for inviting me."

As the night ended, another senator approached us and asked if we had had the opportunity to tour the Rock Islands. When I responded that we had not, he offered his boat and his personal skipper. "I would be honored if you would accept my offer to take my boat out for a day of relaxation and sightseeing," he told us. "We'd love for you to see Peleliu, an island about an hour from here."

"We would love to, but there are 10 of us," I responded.

"No problem! Be at my dock at 8 a.m. on Friday morning. You will have a great day." I thanked him, already looking forward to the trip.

The vice president and his wife then approached us.

"Your story fascinates us," he began. "We are amazed that you were able to heal so completely. It's so exciting that your children have turned out to be healthy adults, as well.

"There are many people who have hurt me with their words," he continued, "and I was not sure I could ever forgive them. But, if you can forgive your attackers for what they have done, surely I can forgive others with God's help. Our country does face many challenges, and we appreciate your help more than you know."

He then turned to Jeremy. "Son, as vice president, I serve as the minister of justice over the criminal system, education system and social family system. There is so much work to be done, and I feel strongly that you could be a wonderful help to me."

Jeremy blinked, obviously flattered and humbled by this amazing offer. "Thank you. I'll do whatever I can," he replied without hesitation.

We also had the privilege to honor the police officer and two village men who had rescued Sherri from the military bunker. I became quite emotional as we shook hands and hugged. "I can't thank you enough for what you did," I told them, tears filling my eyes. "I have never forgotten you. You were like a ray of sunshine in our dark night all those years ago."

By the time the evening ended, we were exhausted but elated. I had no idea we would have the chance to touch so many people, from the lowliest of prisoners to the highest of government officials. We had accomplished so much, and we still had the open-air meetings ahead of us. I prayed that many would turn out in attendance and that God would do a great healing work among the Palauan people.

Thursday was the opening night of our meetings. A worship team had come all the way from Guam to join us for the crusade. They began setting up their equipment while I looked around to see what needed to be done.

I was impressed that so many Palauans had already

stepped in to assure everything would be just right for the big night.

The theme for the three-night crusade was "Soul Survivor." It was based on the program *Survivor: Palau,* which had been filmed on the island several years prior.

During the show, contestants learned to outwit and outlast their opponents. We would talk about how Satan wants to outwit us, outplay us and outlast us to keep us from turning to Jesus. I prayed our theme would be an effective yet fun way to relate to these precious island people.

We had arranged for the crusade to be broadcast on the local radio station and also over the Internet. It seemed we had become almost instant celebrities during our return to the island. Though we sought no publicity, it excited us to think that perhaps our message of forgiveness would reach not just this island, but many people elsewhere, as well. It had been prophesied years prior that our story would reach nations, and now it actually seemed to be happening. What a wonderful opportunity!

"Darrell, do you have a moment?" One of the men from the church strode toward me accompanied by another man. He stopped in front of me and introduced his companion. When I heard his name, I knew that I was looking at one of our attackers. I was looking into the eyes of one of the men who had changed our lives forever. I tried not to let the shock on my face show as I greeted him. Looking to my left, I saw Jadie greeting people. She was coming closer to where we stood. I excused myself for a moment. Pulling her aside, I told her she may want to go the other way and that I was going to talk with one of the men who had attacked us. She turned and walked away.

To my surprise, I felt not a trace of animosity toward this man, only sincere pity. I knew he had spent almost 20 years in prison for his crimes. Judging from the conditions I'd observed at the local prison, I knew this time must have been anything but pleasant.

# RETURN TO PALAU

I returned to the man and knelt in front of him. I began to share with him the grace and mercy of God. I told him God had forgiven my sin and that I had long ago forgiven him and the other men who attacked us. Suddenly, Jeremy, Jadie and Sherri appeared by my side. They immediately came in tune with the situation and joined me in extending heartfelt forgiveness.

His only words to us were, "I am sorry; I was young and foolish."

We rejoiced as a family, knowing that we had truly forgiven this man. We did not feel anything but pity for him. Satan tried not only to destroy us, but him. I prayed for him that he would come to understand and respond to the love and forgiveness of God and that he would learn to walk in God's blessing.

The time neared for the crusade to begin. An estimated 500 Palauans showed up, filing into the bleachers on the track and field. The music began, and the people responded, excitement mounting in our veins. It was so beautiful to see so many eager, hopeful faces. The needs no doubt were as varied as the people. The question was would they be open to the message God had for them?

The high chief sat in the front row with us. We learned he was a Christ follower, and we rejoiced. The chief stood after the singing and addressed the crowd in Palauan. We did not understand most of his words until he spoke in English near the end.

He encouraged the crowd to listen carefully to the message I would bring and respond to it. Responding to this message, the chief asserted, would change their lives for the better. This thrilled me to no end.

Next, Jennifer stood and sang "My Palau." Once again, her song made an enormous impact on the people. They cried, tears spilling down their cheeks as her beautiful words danced upon their hearts.

Truly, God had given Jennifer a rare and beautiful gift.

She had not had a clue the impact her song would make on the Palauans when she first wrote it. She merely knew that God had given her a vision, and she wanted to share it with His precious people.

I stood to speak with great anticipation. Five hundred pairs of eyes were focused on me, awaiting the message for which they had come.

"Thank you all for coming," I began. "I believe God has a special message for you tonight, and I pray you will open your hearts to receive it." Slowly, I relayed our story to them, sharing how we had traveled down the road of forgiveness following the attack. I also shared that, since my arrival in Palau, I had had the opportunity to meet one of our attackers and extend our forgiveness toward him. No one stirred. They sat mesmerized, taking it all in.

At the conclusion of the message, I offered the opportunity for people to respond. "If you would like to ask Jesus to forgive your sins and become the leader of your life, please raise your hand. We would love to pray for you." I looked up and scanned the crowd. My heart soared when almost half the stadium raised their hands! "Please come down so our team can pray with you," I instructed. "If you would like healing, as well, please come down."

One by one, people filed forward, many still speechless, some touched to the point of tears. It was an overwhelming, joyous time. Nothing could have prepared us for such a powerful response to the gospel message.

*Thank You, Lord!*

Nearly 100 people approached us for healing. We made sure to pray for each one. Their stories were amazing. One by one, they shared how they had suffered for years from a variety of ailments, from back pain to heart conditions to hearing problems. One little girl with a totally deaf left ear was healed! We rejoiced as we prayed over them and saw an almost instant healing. Truly, God was in this place tonight! We could only attribute this mighty response to Him!

# RETURN TO PALAU

Morning came again all too soon. I awoke, fully rested. Sleep had not been an issue for us this time around. We pulled on our swimsuits, slathered on the sunscreen and prepared for a wonderful day out on the senator's boat. We were truly humbled and grateful that he had so generously offered us this excursion. It would be a welcome treat after an emotional and exciting few days.

The boat was not your ordinary watercraft. It was a 40-foot vessel powered by two 350-horse turbo diesel engines and had the ability to reach speeds of nearly 60 miles per hour. We stepped in, ready for the ride of our lives.

We sped off toward the most southern tip of Palau, the state of Peleliu. A series of tiny rock islands covered with tropical foliage comprised this spectacular state. During World War II, the state of Peleliu witnessed one of the three bloodiest battles of the war. Invaded by the Japanese and held as a strategic stronghold for refueling and re-arming, I found it fascinating that such a tiny island held so much history.

The vice president met us in Peleliu and presented us each with a special coin that represented his circle of friends. The coin displayed his personal seal on the back.

Then we moved on to snorkeling, which was unlike anything we had ever experienced. It was easy to see why Palau is considered one of the premier diving spots in the world. We spent the afternoon exploring the breathtaking turquoise waters and swimming with the fish. The coral was so brightly colored it astounded me. I felt like I'd been dipped into the world's most exotic aquarium. It was the outing of a lifetime!

Jadie and I had a chance to talk on the boat ride back.

"I have to admit, Dad, the first couple of days, I really didn't want to be here. I knew that I was supposed to be here, but I just wasn't excited. Wednesday evening, however, when we met with all those dignitaries, I began to see the full impact our story had made on people. I began to really pray for God's vision and plan for this week and for the country of

Palau. Now I really feel excited about what God is going to do during the remainder of our trip."

"I'm glad you shared that with me," I said quietly. "What do you see as God's vision and heart for Palau?"

Jadie paused thoughtfully. "The verse Jeremiah 29:11 keeps coming to mind, that God has a hope and a future for this country and wants to bless them. He obviously wants salvation.

"I feel like God gave an opportunity to the last generation of Palau, and they kind of turned it down. But I feel a fresh innocence and spark with this new generation, especially with the few teenagers we've encountered. I see a picture of Palau as innocent and pure, waiting for God to transform it to a place of great peace where His spirit dwells and rests."

"Incredible," I replied, soaking in her words. "I see that, too. A fresh chance for this nation to turn their heart toward God. I pray they do that tonight."

That evening, we held a second crusade. The crowd was not as large, but it was still exciting to see the bleachers filling as we prepared to share. Jeremy served as the main speaker.

He talked this time about current event topics like pornography, media and other things that were relatively new in Palau. He stressed the negative social and spiritual consequences of these things and how we should fight against them.

At one point while he spoke, heavy rain clouds moved in over the field, and it looked as though it might pour. Jeremy kept on preaching, and it began to sprinkle. I knew many needed to hear the message tonight and prayed that God would keep the rain at bay until the service was over.

Suddenly, Jeremy stopped preaching, raised his hand toward the sky and prayed, "Lord, we ask You to hold back the rain until we complete Your business here." Moments after he spoke these words, the rain immediately stopped. We all rejoiced.

After Jeremy's message, many more came forward to give

their hearts to Jesus. It was exciting to see so many fresh faces making the most important decision of their life. Many, we learned, had heard of the miraculous healings of the night before and had come to be healed. One man had received a head injury 29 years before and had been in constant pain. You could see the stress in his eyes. As I prayed, he was immediately freed from the pain. He said, "This is the first time in 29 years that my head has not hurt."

We prayed for everyone and rejoiced again as most were healed. As soon as the time for prayer was finished and we started walking toward the cars, the skies opened and we were soaked to the skin.

The next morning, we received a report that many people had been healed and made a decision for Christ after listening to the radio broadcast. To think that people had simply been driving in their cars or listening from home and received healing or come to Christ was wonderfully exciting! Again, it hit me that we may never truly know the full impact of that week.

Saturday morning, we embarked on another amazing outing, provided by the men's ministry of the church. We were so thankful for an opportunity to experience a leisurely outing following two nights of intense events. Our team and people from the church filled three boats and headed to Jellyfish Lake, where we were able to swim with thousands of non-poisonous jellyfish. Everyone had a blast, especially Bradley and Brandon. They swam off like two little fish themselves!

Saturday night was the final outdoor crusade. Again, hundreds of people showed to hear us speak. Jadie spoke first, then I concluded and invited people forward. Indeed, many more people came to accept Jesus as the Lord and to be healed.

I felt as excited as I had the first night as we stopped to pray for and minister to one person after another.

Looking into their deep brown eyes, I felt a passion for

these Palauans like I had never experienced before. I prayed God's word would return tenfold, that they would go out and share the good news and keep it going.

"My knees are healed!"

"My pain is gone!"

"My arthritis has disappeared!"

These were just a few of the miraculous claims following the service. Each one was like music to my ears, and each time, I rejoiced at how faithful the Lord was. I also prayed for those listening on the radio, that they, too, would be healed.

How exciting to know God was doing a work around the nation as people listened in!

Little Bradley and Brandon were already tucked into bed when we returned to the hotel that night. They were exhausted from the whirlwind of events that week, and Jennifer had stayed behind with them. "How did it go?" she asked, looking up eagerly.

"Let's just say God is moving in ways we could never have dreamed!" I replied, grinning. Then, I realized that our time in Palau was coming to an end. "We still have the church service ahead of us tomorrow before we have to head home. I think we'd better get a good night's sleep!"

"This week definitely flew by," Jennifer agreed. "I'm glad God has an itinerary of His own. I couldn't have imagined things going as smoothly as they did this week. All I can say is WOW!"

Sunday morning, I awoke with a twinge of sadness in my heart. That night, we would be saying goodbye to the land and people we had come to love. God had truly worked in amazing ways. I felt as if I could easily stay another month!

Truly, the Palauans had helped us to feel at home here. I prayed one day we might even get to return again. Already, it seemed the Lord was preparing Jeremy to be used in partnership with the leadership of Palau.

The church was packed to capacity. We each took turns sharing the one thing we had overcome through the years with the Lord's help. I shared on trust, Sherri shared on worthlessness and value, Jadie shared on fear, Jeremy shared on faith in God and Jennifer shared on helping a spouse through prayer.

It appeared our message was very impacting. Once again, people came forward to accept Christ and to be healed. And once again, we felt truly humbled that God had used us as the tools to help these people learn of His love.

That evening, our final church service was more emotional and powerful than I could have ever predicted. We began with a time of singing and testimony. One by one, people came forward to share what God had done in their lives and how they had been healed. The time continued for nearly two hours.

Jeremy spoke about the power of testimony. I was impressed once again with his giftedness in communicating the Bible in simple terms the Palauans could understand. After he finished, we promised the people we would minister to everyone who desired prayer. One by one, they lined up around the entire building. We spent the next hour and a half ministering to them in various ways.

One teenage boy walked through the prayer line on crutches. He had been bitten by a lionfish and had a bad infection in his leg. As he continued through the line, God touched him, and he was instantly healed. He ran to the back of the church holding his crutches over his head. We rejoiced at yet another miracle God had performed!

I could have gone on all night, but we had a plane to catch. With regret, we closed the service in prayer, thanking the Lord for all the wonderful things He had done in the service and during the week. It had been more amazing than words could describe!

After a quick trip to the hotel to gather our belongings, we headed to the airport. Our flight left at 1:45 a.m.

When we arrived at midnight, a large group had gathered to see us off. They had made fresh leis for us and seemed genuinely sad to see us go.

"Come back again!" they cried, embracing us with tears.

"We hope to," I assured them. "This has truly been an experience of a lifetime — one we will never forget."

As I looked up, I noticed several men and women in the uniforms of airport employees. I recognized them as having just been in the church service. A smile crept to my lips as I realized just how "small" a world it truly is.

To think we had had a chance to share with everyone from prisoners to government officials to airport employees! What a blessing.

As we boarded the plane back to Guam, exhaustion swept over all of us.

"This is the longest day of my life!" Bradley exclaimed.

I laughed. "And it's not over yet! We still have to fly to Hawaii. Do you realize that with the time change, our day will actually be twice as long? So it really is the longest day of your life."

A myriad of emotions swept over me as the plane lifted off. I turned to Sherri and squeezed her hand. "Well, can you believe it's over?" I whispered.

She shook her head wearily. "No. It seems we just flew in yesterday. God is so good, Darrell! So much has happened this week, I feel as if it has been a year! I'm not ready to go. I am so thankful we had the chance to share with as many people as we did. And who knows how many more were touched by listening in on the radio."

I nodded. "We may never know the impact this side of heaven. Something tells me our story of Palau is far from over."

As Palau became a tiny dot below us, I thanked the Lord once again for bringing our story full circle. What a wonderful testimony to the power of God and His faithfulness! A peace filled my soul as Ephesians 3:20 came to mind once again: "Now to Him who is able to do immeasurably more than all we ask or imagine."

Indeed, our week had been infinitely more blessed than we could have ever imagined.

*Thank You, Lord. We could not have asked for more!*

# Chapter Nine
# WHAT WE HAVE LEARNED

## Darrell

It was difficult for me to find a way to weave what I have learned over many years into the storyline of this book. I do, however, believe that what I learned was of great value and was the key to our healing process. I want to share these truths with you.

I have always known that my choices were very important. I have always tried to make good choices, knowing that if I trusted in God and obeyed His word, everything would work out for my good.

My choice was something that I could control. I could not, however, control the choices of others. I could share truth and the consequences of poor choices, hoping to influence people to make right choices. But I could not choose for them.

Little did I realize the impact that the wrong choices of others would have on my life and the life of my family. Dealing with the consequences of the wrong choices of others suddenly became a way of life for me.

It would have been easy to become bitter. However, it was important that I affected my family with the consequences of my right choices. If I made the choice to become bitter and angry and allowed myself to get depressed, they would have had a poor example to follow and no doubt, they would have followed my lead. I had to make good choices that would produce a positive outcome. I had to lead by what I knew to be true and not by what I felt.

I felt like a failure as a father. I had not been able to protect them. But I also knew that I had done everything I could, that I was even willing to give my life for them. I had to let what I knew motivate me and not what I felt. Now I had to do everything in my power to be an example of doing the right thing. I would not allow us to take on a victim mentality. I would not allow what had happened to us dictate who we would become. My response to what happened would be the deciding factor. I chose well; I chose to forgive and to lead my family in forgiveness.

Choosing to forgive the individuals who harmed us was not a difficult choice for me. It was the right choice.

Coming to understand the reality of what forgiveness really is was more difficult. Knowing about forgiveness and walking in forgiveness can be as opposite as night and day. It was not that I did not want to walk in forgiveness. I did. It was coming to understand the reality of what forgiveness is and then putting what I learned into practice that took time.

During and following the attack, I had to deal with feelings that I had not dealt with before. I hated what was done to us and those who caused it. I wanted revenge. I wanted them to experience the fear and pain we experienced. I wanted them dead.

I will never forget the feelings I experienced that day at the trial when I stood feet from my attacker on the veranda. I wanted so badly to grab the pistol of the officer and become judge and jury. I am grateful to God that I did not allow these feelings to control my actions.

I knew what the Bible said. "'Vengeance is mine,' says the Lord, 'I will repay.'" "Do not pay back evil for evil." "Love your enemies." I chose to allow what I knew to be the motivation for my actions and not what I felt. I am so glad I had learned this lesson.

I never did feel like forgiving, but it was something Jesus said I was to do. For me, **forgiveness was a choice and not a feeling**. It was an obedience issue. It was something I could do. As a child of God, it was a **command and not an option**.

God brought many scriptures to life for me as I searched for answers. It is so important to understand the truth of God's word and apply it to life's circumstances. We can rest assured that when we know the truth and apply that truth, the truth will set us free. I cannot here explore in depth all the scriptures that helped me. But I do want to list some of them:

Ephesians 6:10-13: It is important to know the enemy.

John 10:10: It is important to understand the enemy's purpose so we can recognize his activity.

2 Corinthians 2:10-11: Satan desires to outwit us in the area of unforgiveness.

Ephesians 4:26-27: Satan desires to get a foothold or a stronghold in our life so he can influence us.

John 14:30-31: The enemy had no hold on Jesus. I don't want him to have any hold on me, either, especially because of unforgiveness.

Luke 23:34: Jesus asked the Father to forgive the people who had crucified Him prior to their asking.

Acts 7:60: Stephen prayed as he was being stoned, "Lord, do not hold this sin against them." He understood the power of forgiveness.

Matthew 6:12, 14: Our forgiveness is tied to our willingness to forgive.

Matthew18:21-35: If this is how my heavenly Father will treat me, I choose to forgive from the heart.

Matthew 5:23-25 and Mark 11:25: God wants us to be right with men so we can be right with Him.

1 John 4:19-21: Loving those we can see is a prerequisite to loving a God we can't see.

2 Corinthians 10:4-5: Our spiritual weapons are powerful enough to demolish the strongholds and lies of the enemy.

I read a lot in my quest to find answers. One book that really helped me was Neil Anderson's book *The Bondage Breaker*. My understanding of forgiveness was influenced greatly by his writings and is reflected in the principles that I share.

# WHAT WE HAVE LEARNED

I believe that one of the biggest blockages to forgiveness is a wrong understanding of who benefits from it. If our understanding is that forgiveness benefits the offender, we may be hesitant to forgive.

Why would I want to do anything that would benefit someone who has hurt me? Our natural thinking is that if we don't forgive, we will have the power to hold something over the person who harmed us and in some way, cause him or her to suffer as he or she caused us to suffer.

In reality, however, unforgiveness keeps us attached to the offending person. Unforgiveness gives the enemy of our souls an open doorway to our thoughts through which he can continue to steal our sleep and our peace. I was really grateful to come to understand that **forgiveness is for the benefit of the offended and not the offender**. It breaks the attachments the enemy has on my thoughts. This truth was a key to my recovery.

I knew I was supposed to forgive the people who had harmed me. And I did pray and said that I forgave them. My struggle came as I continued to lose sleep at night, reliving the events over and over again. I felt angry and even guilty for taking my family to Palau in the first place. Every time a memory of what took place was triggered, there was pain. With the pain came the ongoing struggle not to be fearful or angry, or unforgiving. I was not purposefully choosing to be unforgiving. But I was missing something. Every time the pain came, I would hear the lies of the enemy saying, "You haven't forgiven." Since I was still dealing with the memories, I assumed that I had not forgiven, even though it was my desire to do so. Believing this lie kept me entangled.

What really helped me was coming to understand that forgiveness is more than a one-time event. The action that caused the need for forgiveness may have happened once, or it may have taken place over days, weeks, months or years. But the act of forgiveness only begins when you choose to forgive. I have learned that **forgiveness is a process, not an**

**event**. When I choose to forgive, I begin a journey of forgiveness.

Every time a memory was triggered and I experienced pain, I would hear the enemy say, "You have not forgiven." With my new understanding, I no longer agreed with him.

I responded by declaring truth: "I did forgive, and I choose to continue to forgive." Rejoicing, I realized that my journey of forgiveness concerning what happened to my family in Palau was complete.

## Sherri

Friedrich Nietzsche, the philosopher, said, "What doesn't kill us makes us stronger."

I would probably say, "If we respond well, we can become stronger."

We have tried for many years to put our thoughts concerning the lessons learned and changes in our lives onto the printed page. The healing process for each member of our family was as different as our painful experiences and personalities. There were a couple of things we all held in common, however.

The foremost struggle for us all was an unwillingness to be separated. It is a normal thing for parents to want to know the whereabouts of their children, but our kids had the same concerns for us. Satan had tried to destroy our family, and he used lies to try to bring us to desperation.

During the night of our attack, each had been told that the others would be killed and that he or she would be left to struggle alone. It took us some time to get over such a psychological blow and recognize that history does not always repeat itself. Over time, we saw that we could still trust God with our loved ones, even when we were not with them ourselves.

We all also struggled to some degree with fear of the dark. It didn't take long to realize that the source of that fear came from our inability to turn on a light when we had desperately needed to. Having electricity at our disposal made all the difference in dispelling a fear that the enemy had tried to use for our demise.

Personally, I found myself struggling with things that I had never felt before:

1. First and most surprising to me was my intense anger. I had never really dealt with this emotion before this time. My past experience with the anger of others had been a painful effort. Now that I was feeling this emotion intensely myself, it was sometimes overwhelming. I had to learn that we all experience anger in some measure, but some of us internalize that feeling. The Bible talks a good deal about this subject. Ephesians 4:26-27, 29 says, "In your anger do not sin: do not let the sun go down while you are still angry. Do not give the devil a foothold. Do not let any unwholesome talk come out of your mouths, but only what is helpful for building others up according to their needs, that it may benefit those who listen."

With some effort and much prayer, I actually became a healthier person after coming through that struggle. Once more, the enemy of our souls (Satan) lost in his battle to "steal, kill and destroy" (John 10:10).

2. I do not want to overlook the struggles I had in overcoming the damage done to my heart and soul by the abuse I endured that night. So many women in our culture are similarly abused. They are told to "get over it" or "it was no big deal." But there is a grieving time and healing process that must be honored. Darrell was diligent in learning how "my problem" was really "our problem." His help was invaluable to my becoming a whole person again.

3. Fear was something I had conquered many times throughout my past. I was frustrated to have that "unwelcome stranger" weasel its way back into my life again and attempt to take up permanent residence there. I had tried before to will my way out of fear or to talk myself

beyond its grip. The truth is, only one thing really brought me freedom; I had to rebuke that foul spirit and renounce its hold on me. Wisdom also told me that it would be helpful to limit fear's opportunities to return. We were diligent about carefully choosing the things we saw and heard through movies and television. No sense in creating additional reasons to fear.

4. The death of our dreams took me a long time to reconcile in my mind. Eventually, we had to leave missions. The choices of our attackers had directly affected our lives and our future in what seemed to be a negative way. I really had to depend on Romans 8:28.

Each of the above difficulties fell behind me as time went on. I believe that time can be the healer of all wounds, but only when we are constantly following the truth of the scripture, desiring to become more like Jesus. Our natural reactions are usually contrary to the spiritually minded responses that God wants from us. We must "take captive every thought to make it obedient to Christ" (2 Corinthians 10:5b). An old adage says that trouble will make us bitter or better. We chose "better."

## Jeremy

Through forgiveness comes trust, love and intimacy.

*Forgiveness* is not an event but a choice and a process. It does not make the wrong done to you okay, but it releases your hands from the throat of the one who has harmed you. In doing so, you also release the spiritual hold that he or she has on you that the enemy uses to torment you. That's the reason forgiveness is a process.

The enemy will continue to try to remind you and torment you. The first few days, you may have to forgive 100 times or more. But it will get easier as time goes on. Remember that the Father is our strength, our peace, our joy and even loving Him is a choice.

# WHAT WE HAVE LEARNED

Forgiveness doesn't mean that you can't be angry or even shouldn't be angry. You can actually be angry and still live in forgiveness, because what was done to you was not okay and it was wrong. But do not sin in your anger or take justice or revenge into your own hands. Unforgiveness demands justice and revenge from our own hands. True forgiveness releases justice and revenge to the Father and allows you to trust the Father with the outcome.

Forgiveness is complete when you can remember the event and there is no more pain. You may still experience emotion from time to time or even anger on occasion. But there will not be any pain in your heart from the memory. At that point, you will actually desire freedom and restoration for the person who harmed you, because you will see him or her through the love of the Father, not through your own pain.

*Trust* cannot be realized, achieved or really even understood in its fullness until forgiveness has taken place.

For many years, I was angry with God for what happened to me and my family. I knew it wasn't His fault and He didn't cause it to happen, but I was angry that He didn't intervene. I didn't even realize I was angry with Him.

As a result, my anger led to a lack of trust. I trusted God once, and it nearly killed my family. I chose to be obedient and to serve Him, but not to trust Him. This type of behavior shaped the way I arranged and lived my adult life, too. I would seek God's will and then set up my own plan that I knew I could make happen, a way that would be safe. I didn't trust many people, either. I became a super overachiever, doing it all myself while still being obedient and serving God — not as an intimate lover of Him, not pursuing a closer relationship with Him, not even as a friend, but as a slave.

In prayer, the Holy Spirit showed me that I was angry with the Father and needed to forgive Him. In an amazing experience of His love, I gladly did so, and my whole perspective of reality changed. I could once again know trust and chose to trust my loving Father in heaven with the deepest parts of my soul. I was finally able to see Him as the lover of my soul.

*Love.* Have you ever thought about the fact that we love some people out of obligation, but don't trust them and certainly don't like them? This comes up a lot with family — the whole "you can choose your friends, but not your family" cliché. In that perspective, is it really love or just a mutual tolerance? As Christians, we say, "Of course I love God." But do we really understand what it means to love Him? If we don't trust someone, there is no way we can truly love him or her.

For many years, I maintained a wrong understanding of the character of God. My problem went something like this: How do I love a God who I don't trust? How can I trust a God who didn't take care of me and protect me when I was hurting? Perspective is reality, and it is a powerful thing.

Much of the Bible gives us examples of God's character. But if we miss the point of why Jesus came, then we miss everything. Yes, Jesus came to die on the cross and forgive our sins. But why? To restore the ability for us to have a relationship with the Father, Jesus and the Holy Spirit!

Just like Adam and Eve in the Garden of Eden, Father God is longing for you to know Him the way Jesus knows Him. He's a good God. There is no evil in Him, only good! He is the safest place to love. He loves us so much that He allowed Jesus to pay the price so that we could know true love in Him.

Jesus was willing because He, too, loves us and longs for us to have a relationship with the Father, as well as Himself. This relationship is made possible through the Holy Spirit, whom Jesus gave us as our Comforter and Teacher. The Holy Spirit is the part of the Trinity here on earth with us. He dwells in you and longs to introduce you to the Father and Jesus as they truly are, not as the world or your experience tells you.

Loving God in true love means trusting Him with all of you and all that is precious to you. How do you get to know a friend or potential spouse? By having a relationship with him or her, by spending time together. The more time we spend with God, the more we share with Him, the more of life we go through with Him, the more our love and passion for Him grows.

*Intimacy* is a result of commitment, passion, love and trust, all of which you cannot have without forgiveness. It's a crazy cycle that can catch us and distract us for years from what the Father longs for.

### Jadie

"Time heals all." For me, that saying was about as far from the truth as "sticks and stones may break my bones, but words will never hurt me."

What I have learned is this: Time + Conflict = Change. King David is a great example of this. 2 Samuel 3:1 says, "The war between the house of Saul and the house of David lasted a long time. David grew stronger and stronger while the house of Saul grew weaker and weaker."

The key is David was seeking God, and Saul was seeking revenge. What you choose to do with the conflict in your life is what will determine the kind of change you experience.

Romans 8:28 tell us, "And we know that all things work together for good to them that love God, to them who are the called according to His purpose."

God has a plan for our lives. Jeremiah 29:11 says, "'For I know the plans I have for you,' declares the Lord, 'plans to prosper you and not to harm you, plans to give you hope and a future.'"

Satan also has a plan for your life.

1 Peter 5:8 warns us: "Be self-controlled and alert. Your enemy the devil prowls around like a roaring lion looking for someone to devour." So "when the day of evil comes" (Ephesians 6:13), run to the one who can save you

and not to the one who is trying to devour you!

There is so much to tell and countless milestones along the way to share. The experience of writing this book with my family has prompted me to continue another book I started long ago that goes even deeper into the spiritual journey God has walked me through over the years — a journey that has led me into the arms of my God.

What He has produced in me is, as Jeremiah says, "a fire shut up in my bones." It's a story longing to be told in its entirety.

Isaiah 61:1-3 refers to the captive being set free. Jesus set me free from my prison of fear and shame, and in doing so, handed me the keys, commissioning me to do the same for as many as will listen! I pray that the words of this book will bring you hope and set you on a journey to complete freedom in Christ.

As you read this, pray for me, also, that God will continue to stir in me the "rest of the story."

> "Be anxious for nothing, but in everything by prayer and supplication, with thanksgiving, let your requests be made known to God; and the peace of God, which surpasses all understanding, will guard your hearts and minds through Christ Jesus." (Philippians 4:6-7)

# CONCLUSION

No one ever wishes to be a victim of violent crime or to have to deal with tragic events like disease or accidents. But the truth is we live in a sinful world where bad things happen to good people.

People get hurt, and hurt people hurt people. And sadly, it's not if, but when. Yet how we respond to hurtful people and circumstances will determine if we live an angry, bitter life of bondage or a life of peace and freedom. Our choice will determine if we become bitter or better.

I learned at an early age that I was born with a sin-bent nature. No one ever taught me to lie, cheat or be selfish. It was inborn. Because of our sin-bent nature, people say and do things that hurt others.

As I grew older, I learned that this sin nature was the result of the disobedience of Adam and Eve. The penalty for their sin included physical and spiritual death, for them and all people to come. That was the bad news.

The good news was that Jesus, God's Son, died on the cross to pay the price for my sin. When I came to understand this truth, I asked Jesus to forgive me for the wrong I had done to others and for the wrong I had done to Him.

Since Jesus had already paid for my sin, there was no reason not to accept His provision. I asked Jesus to forgive my sin and to come and lead my life.

This began my lifelong journey of following Biblical truth and doing my best to become like Jesus. It was on this journey of faith that I had the opportunity to put into practice what I had learned about forgiveness.

God had freely extended His forgiveness to my family and me. We needed to freely extend our forgiveness to our attackers.

The first step to being able to reap the benefits of forgiveness is to deal with your own sin: the ways you have wronged others and the ways you have wronged God. Ask God to forgive you and to apply the provision of His Son, Jesus, to your life. You may want to use the following prayer:

*Dear Heavenly Father,*

*I know that I have sinned against others, and I have sinned against You. I ask You to forgive my sin. Please apply the provision of Your Son, Jesus, to my life. I choose to trust in Him for my eternal life. I now trust in Jesus to be the leader and Lord of my life. In Jesus' name, amen.*

The next step is to choose to forgive those who have hurt you. Unforgiveness gives the enemy a foothold, a stronghold in your life. His desire is to weigh you down and influence you in such a way that you stay angry, bitter and in bondage. That is no way to live. Forgiveness brings you freedom from the ongoing assault of the enemy. I encourage you to pray this prayer:

*Dear Jesus,*

*In obedience to Your word, I choose now to enter this journey of forgiveness. Please forgive me for the times I have hurt others and for my unwillingness to forgive those who have hurt me. I choose now to forgive (verbalize who you are forgiving) for what he or she has said or done to me (verbalize what this person did and how it made you feel). I now bring the blood of Jesus Christ between me and what was said or done to me, forever closing the doorway of unforgiveness. Thank You, Jesus, for Your forgiveness, freedom and peace. Amen.*

Remember:
Forgiveness is a command, not an option.
Forgiveness is a choice and not a feeling.

# CONCLUSION

Forgiveness is for your benefit and not the benefit of the offender.

Forgiveness is a process, not an event.

I trust that you have learned from our life story. May you always walk in forgiveness, freedom and peace.

# CONTACT INFORMATION

Darrell and Sherri Beebe travel fulltime,
sharing their message of hope, healing and forgiveness.

The Beebes can be reached through their website at
www.darknessatdawn.info
or by mail at:
D.L. Beebe Ministries
PO Box 397
Mossyrock, WA 98564

Additional books can be purchased through the website.

Jeremy and his wife, Jennifer,
are evangelists and mentors and can be reached at
jeremy.beebe@gmail.com

Jadie and her husband, David,
are senior pastors in Indiana and can be reached at
jadiehager@yahoo.com

# GOOD CATCH
# PUBLISHING

www.goodcatchpublishing.com